INSOMNIACS INC.

VOL. 1

THE AWAKENING

TRACEY ROBINSON

ISBN: 978-1-7361198-1-5

This book was printed in the United States of America

To order additional copies of this book contact:

LaBoo Publishing Enterprise, LLC
staff@laboopublishing.com
www.laboopublishing.com

TABLE OF CONTENTS

TRACEY ROBINSON

INTRODUCTION

Share my experience as I write the words I hear from the spirits both near and far, thanking you in advance for the opportunity all of you have given me, nurturing the 'art-form' I've been longing to release: with this my first publication as a freshman author.

I THANK YOU

TRACEY 'PRINCE' ROBINSON

I'M AN INSOMNIAC

TO ANYONE WHO SITS ALONE,
AND FEELS IN GREAT DESPAIR,
WHO HAS NO ONE TO TURN TO AND
WHO THINKS THAT NO ONE CARES.
TO EVERY CHILD WHO THINKS NO ONE
HEARS WHAT THEY HAVE TO SAY,
WHO'S COME TO THE CONCLUSION THAT
IT'S TIME TO RUN AWAY.
TO EVERYONE WHO'S RUN AWAY,
AND WANTS TO GO BACK HOME,
FOR ONCE OUT IN THE WORLD THEY LEARNED,
THEY WERE NEVER ALONE.
TO EVERYONE WHO HARBORS THOUGHTS,
OF THEIR OWN SUICIDE,
WHO MAY HAVE NO SENSE OF SELF-WORTH,
AND LOST ALL THOUGHTS OF PRIDE.
TO EVERYONE ABOUT TO TAKE
THAT FIRST, LONG DRAG OF CRACK,
WHO KNOWS THEIR SOUL WILL SOON TURN COLD,
FOR THERE'S NO TURNING BACK.
TO EVERYONE WHO'S GRABBED A GUN,

TO SETTLE SOME ODD SCORE,
WHEN BULLETS FLY,
SOME MAY SURVIVE,
AND SOME MAY LIVE NO MORE.
TO EVERYONE WHO'S STANDING HIGH,
ALONE AND ON A LEDGE,
ABOUT TO CLOSE THEIR EYES AND JUST
STEP FAR OUT FROM THE EDGE.
TO EVERY YOUNG WOMAN,
WHO LEFT HOME JUST TO DANCE,
WHO HAS BEEN USED,
AND SITS CONFUSED,
AND WANTS ANOTHER CHANCE.
TO EVERY ONE OF YOU I SAY,
THERE IS A BETTER WAY,
YOU CAN SURVIVE YOUR CIRCUMSTANCE,
YOU CAN LIVE THROUGH THE DAY.
I'VE LIVED A LIFE OF SUFFERING,
AND I HAVE FELT GREAT PAIN,
AND EACH TIME THAT I TRIED TO RISE,
I FELL BACK DOWN AGAIN.
I'VE HARBORED THOUGHTS OF MURDER AND
CONSIDERED SUICIDE,
I FELT NO LEVEL OF SELF-WORTH,
AND I HAD LOST ALL PRIDE.
I LIVED LIKE SOME WILD ANIMAL,

TRACEY ROBINSON

LOCKED UP WITHIN A CAGE,
SURROUNDED BY SO MANY MEN,
OUR HEARTS ALL FILLED WITH RAGE.
BUT SOMEWHERE, SOMEHOW,
ON SOME DAY, I DON'T REMEMBER WHEN,
AN EVENT OCCURRED WITHIN ME AND
A SUDDEN CHANGE BEGAN.
I LOOKED BACK ON MY LIFE AND I
LOOKED AT THINGS DIFFERENTLY,
I SAW ALL OF THE BLESSINGS THAT
HAD BEEN BESTOWED ON ME.
I THOUGHT ABOUT MY CHILDREN,
MY LIVING TREASURE CHEST,
I THOUGHT OF HOW,
WHEN I GOT SHOT,
I WAS SAVED BY MY VEST.
I THOUGHT OF ALL THE INCIDENTS
I MANAGED TO SURVIVE,
AND HOW LUCKY I TRULY AM
THAT I AM STILL ALIVE.
I FELT THE HANDS OF ANGELS,
WHICH YANKED ME TO AND FRO,
REMOVING ME FROM EACH SPOT THAT
A BULLET MEANT TO GO.
I THOUGHT OF ALL THE FRIENDS I KNOW,
AND WHAT IT WAS THEY'D SAY,

IF I SELFISHLY MADE A CHOICE
WHICH TOOK MY LIFE AWAY.
I THOUGHT ABOUT THE WAYS THAT I
WOULD ALWAYS HELP THE WEAK,
PERHAPS THAT'S WHY
THE SPIRITS CHOSE
FOR ME TO HEAR THEM SPEAK.
IF I CAN TURN MY LIFE AROUND,
THEN SO CAN ALL OF YOU,
REGARDLESS OF HOW YOU HAVE LIVED,
OR WHAT YOU HAVE BEEN THROUGH.
I FEEL YOU AND I CANNOT SLEEP,
I'M AN INSOMNIAC,
IF YOU GIVE UP, THE WORLD WOULD LOSE
A SOUL IT CAN'T GET BACK.
FOR ALL OF YOU ABOUT TO LEAVE,
PLEASE JUST DECIDE TO STAY.
GATHER YOUR STRENGTH SO YOU CAN FACE
A NEW AND BETTER DAY.
TO EVERYONE WHO'S GONE AWAY,
AND WANTS TO COME BACK HOME,
TRY TO REACH OUT AND CLOSE THAT GAP,
PLEASE JUST PICK UP THE PHONE.
DON'T TAKE A SINGLE SAMPLE
OF SOME ADDICTIVE DRUG;
YOUR CHILD SITS ANXIOUSLY AT HOME,

TRACEY ROBINSON

JUST YEARNING FOR YOUR HUG.
TO THOSE OF YOU WHO ONCE THOUGHT WRONG,
JUST THINK OF WHAT IS RIGHT,
SO THAT SO MANY MOTHERS MAY
SLEEP SOUNDLY THROUGH THE NIGHT.
I SOMETIMES SEE THE SPIRITS,
THEY WHISPER IN MY EAR,
THEY SAY THAT YOU WILL BE ALRIGHT,
IF YOU JUST HAVE NO FEAR.

I FEEL THE SPIRITS

I'VE BECOME A RECEPTOR
OF LIFE'S PURE ENERGY,
MANY OF THE FEELINGS YOU EXPRESS
ALSO PASS RIGHT THROUGH ME.
I HEAR VOICES OF SPIRITS,
I WALK AMONG THE DEAD,
I SIT DOWN AND I WRITE TO YOU
THE THINGS THAT THEY HAVE SAID.
I WALK AMONG THE SHADOWS,
I BASK WITHIN THE LIGHT,
I CRY FOR THAT WHICH MAN DOES WRONG,
AND PRAISE WHAT MAN DOES RIGHT.
I OFTEN FEEL YOUR SADNESS,
I FLOAT UPON ITS WAVE,
I SEE THE HURT YOU CAN'T FORGET,
AND THAT WHICH YOU FORGAVE.
SOMETIMES I THINK I'M DREAMING,
AND SO I MUST ASK YOU,
"WOULD YOU BELIEVE IN A DREAM,
IF I TOLD YOU THAT IT'S TRUE?"
I'VE SEEN THE EBB OF MANKIND'S TIDE,

TRACEY ROBINSON

AND I HAVE SEEN ITS FLOOD,
I'VE WITNESSED HOW KIND MAN CAN BE,
AND I'VE SEEN MAN SHED BLOOD.
I WALK THE ROAD OF LIFE ALONE,
I FEEL THE MORNING BREEZE,
SOMETIMES IT SEEMS I CANNOT SEE,
THE FOREST FOR THE TREES.
I HEAR THE GROWL OF MONSTERS,
THEY HIDE JUST OUT OF SIGHT,
WAITING FOR THE SUN TO FALL
SO THEY MAY FEED AT NIGHT.
I FEEL THE PAIN OF CHILDREN,
THE PASSING OF THE SOULS;
MY HEART IS SMASHED
LIKE WAVES WHICH CRASH
FIERCELY AGAINST THE SHOALS.
I KNOW THAT I HAVE TOUCHED YOU,
I KNOW I'VE MADE YOU THINK,
I KNOW WE'VE CLIMBED A MOUNTAIN,
AND WE'VE STOOD UPON ITS BRINK.
I'VE BECOME A RECEPTOR,
OF LIFE'S PURE ENERGY;
I FEEL THE SPIRITS,
AND THE THINGS
THAT THEY WHISPER TO ME.

BEFORE THE NIGHT IS THROUGH

SOMEWHERE A MONSTER SITS AT HOME,
THE WAY I'M SITTING NOW,
IT WANTS TO FEED QUITE BADLY BUT
IT MUST FIGURE OUT HOW.
WHILE I LISTEN TO WHISPERS,
AND WRITE DOWN WHAT THEY SAY,
IT LISTENS TO THE DEMONS WHICH
DEMAND IT RAPE AND SLAY.
WHILE I GO TO THE KITCHEN,
TO MAKE MYSELF A SNACK,
A MONSTER TAKES A WALK OUTSIDE,
TO SEE WHOM TO ATTACK.
WE BOTH REFLECT THE OPPOSITES
OF LIFE AND WHAT IT MEANS,
A CLEAR EXAMPLE THAT ALL THINGS
ARE NOT QUITE LIKE THEY SEEM.
SOMEWHERE A MONSTER'S GETTING DRESSED,
AND I AM DRESSING TOO.
IT HOPES TO FIND A VICTIM AND
I KNOW WHAT I MUST DO.

TRACEY ROBINSON

THE MONSTER PACKS ITS WEAPONS,
A KNIFE USUALLY;
I HAVE BEAR SPRAY AND A BATON,
AND MYA WALKS WITH ME.
THE MONSTER MOVES WITH CONFIDENCE,
FOR IT WILL EAT TODAY!
BUT IT DOES NOT KNOW THAT I HUNT,
AND MONSTERS ARE MY PREY.
PERHAPS WE'LL MEET UPON THE STREET,
AND WE MAY GET A CHANCE
TO SEE WHO WILL SURVIVE THE NIGHT,
AFTER DEATH'S DEADLY DANCE.
I SMELL THE EVIL IN THE AIR,
AM I A MONSTER TOO?
AFTER I SLAY ONE SHOULD I FEEL
THE PLEASURE THAT I DO?
IF I FIND MYSELF DRENCHED IN BLOOD,
WHAT DIFFERENCE DOES IT MAKE,
IF IT'S JUST MONSTERS THAT I HUNT,
AND THOSE WHOSE LIVES I TAKE?
WHEN I GO OUT AND LISTEN FOR
THE SCREAM OF THOSE IN NEED,
AM I REALLY USING THEM,
SO THAT I TOO MAY FEED?
PERHAPS IT'S LIKE IN NATURE:
BOTH PREDATOR AND PREY

MAY SOMETIMES HAVE THEIR ROLES REVERSED,
ON ANY GIVEN DAY.
I AM A MONSTER SLAYER,
DEFINED BY WHAT I DO;
I HOPE TO TAKE A MONSTER'S LIFE,
BEFORE THE NIGHT IS THROUGH.

CAIN AND ABLE

HERE IS A TALE OF TWO YOUNG MEN,
BOTH BORN ON THE SAME DAY;
ABLE WAS BORN ON ONE SIDE OF TOWN,
AND CAIN NOT FAR AWAY.
NOW ABLE WAS A BOLD YOUNG KID,
AND KNOWN FOR ACTING OUT,
WHILE MAKING PLANS FOR COLLEGE,
WAS WHAT CAIN WAS ALL ABOUT.
ABLE WANTED ACTION,
HE HUNTED THE NEXT THRILL,
IT WOULD COME AS NO BIG SURPRISE,
WHEN ONE DAY HE WOULD KILL.
CAIN WAS JUST THE OPPOSITE:
HE CARRIED HIMSELF WELL,
ONE LOOK AND YOU KNEW HE'D GO FAR,
INSIDE YOU COULD JUST TELL.
WHILE ABLE SPENT HIS HIGH SCHOOL YEARS
GOING IN AND OUT OF JAIL,
CAIN WHIZZED THROUGH ALL HIS STUDIES,
NOT ONE CLASS DID HE FAIL!
THE NEXT THREE YEARS FOR ABLE

WERE SPENT BEHIND THE WALL.
HE'D STEPPED ON UP TO ROBBERY,
AND FOR THAT HE TOOK A FALL.
CAIN FINISHED COLLEGE EARLY,
AND WAS ALREADY EMPLOYED,
HAD A GIRLFRIEND AND A FAMILY,
AND A LIFE THAT HE ENJOYED.
ONE RAINY NIGHT FIVE YEARS LATER,
CAIN HAD MISSED HIS BUS,
AND AS HE SOUGHT TO CATCH A CAB,
HE THOUGHT OF ALL THE FUSS
HIS WIFE WOULD MAKE CAUSE HE WAS LATE:
IT WAS THEIR SON'S BIRTHDAY,
THEY'D PROMISED HIM A PARTY,
AND HOURS MORE OF PLAY.
CAIN PASSED A DARKENED ALLEYWAY,
AND FROM IT STEPPED A MAN.
THROUGH THE RAIN CAIN LOOKED AND SAW,
A GUN WAS IN HIS HAND.
THE MAN WAS ABLE, AND THOUGH THE TWO
HAD NEVER MET BEFORE,
IT SEEMS THEIR PATHS WERE MEANT TO CROSS,
PREDICTED LONG BEFORE.
CAIN RAISED HIS HAND AS IF TO SAY,
"I WANT NO TROUBLE, SIR,
I'LL GLADLY GIVE YOU ALL I HAVE,

TRACEY ROBINSON

JUST GO ON AS YOU WERE."
BUT ABLE THOUGHT THAT WHEN HIS HAND
CAME UP HE HELD A GUN,
AND ABLE QUICKLY FIRED,
AND THEN HE TURNED TO RUN.
AS CAIN FELL DOWN HE HIT HIS HEAD,
WHICH TURNED HIM TO THE RIGHT,
AND IT WAS THERE THAT HE WOULD SEE
HIS LAST AND FINAL SIGHT.
HE SAW THAT ABLE HAD BEEN SHOT;
A COP HAD BEEN NEARBY,
BOTH CAIN AND ABLE DIED THAT NIGHT,
BOTH LOOKING TOWARD THE SKY.

'DEAD' WHISPERS

I HEAR THE SPIRITS' WHISPERS;
THEY SPEAK WITHIN MY HEAD.
ALTHOUGH THEIR WORDS ARE CRYSTAL CLEAR,
THEY'RE SPOKEN BY THE DEAD.
IT SEEMS THAT THEY HAVE CHOSEN ME,
THEIR LIVING SOUNDING BOARD,
FOR OTHERS MAY HEAR THEM AS WELL,
THOUGH THEY MAY BE IGNORED.
I HARDLY EVER SLEEP AT NIGHT,
THOUGH EVERY NIGHT I TRY,
I'LL NAP AWHILE AND LOOK TO LEARN
THAT LITTLE TIME'S GONE BY.
THE VOICES HAVE THEIR BENEFITS,
LOOK HOW MANY I HAVE TOUCHED,
THE LOVE I'VE BEEN SHOWN IN RETURN,
WHICH MEANS SO VERY MUCH.
I WONDER WHAT WILL HAPPEN
WHEN I HAVE PASSED AWAY,
HOW WILL THEY CHOOSE WITH WHOM TO SPEAK?
WHAT WILL THEY HAVE TO SAY?
WHOEVER THAT PERSON MAY BE,

TRACEY ROBINSON

I HOPE THAT THEY CAN TELL
AMONG THE VOICES THAT THEY HEAR
WILL BE MY VOICE AS WELL.

DEATH'S DEFINED

YOU'VE SEEN WHAT IS MY BLESSING,
NOW KNOW WHAT IS MY CURSE:
I OFTEN FEEL THE PAIN OF SOULS,
AND SOMETIMES, EVEN WORSE,
I FEEL THE PAIN OF CHILDREN.
ITS VENOM BURNS THROUGH ME.
I SOMETIMES SEE THE LAST THINGS THAT
A VICTIM EVER SEES.
I FEEL A WAVE WASH OVER ME,
I DROWN A THOUSAND TIMES,
WHEN MONSTERS FEED,
AND VICTIMS BLEED,
AND DEATH'S AGAIN DEFINED.

TRACEY ROBINSON

GOD CRIED FOR ME

SOMETIMES COURAGE CAN MEAN MUCH MORE
THAN NOT BEING AFRAID.
APOLOGIES ARE GREATER THAN
MISTAKES WE MAY HAVE MADE.
SOME PEOPLE GO THROUGH LIFE AS IF
IT WAS SOME SORT OF GAME.
SOME ARE ABUSED,
AND SOME ACCUSED,
WHILE OTHERS TAKE NO BLAME.
THE STARS THAT GLITTER IN THE SKY,
THEY SPEAK OF WORLDS AWAY,
WHILE OUR NEON TECHNOLOGY
SPEAKS VOLUMES WE DON'T SAY.
I SIT BEFORE AN OCEAN,
I CLOSE MY EYES AND PRAY,
THAT THE FOOTPRINTS I LEFT IN THE SAND
ARE NOT SOON WASHED AWAY.
I'VE TAKEN MANY LOSSES,
AND CHERISHED WHAT I'VE GAINED,
I'VE BASKED IN GOD'S BRIGHT SUNSHINE AND
BEEN PUMMELED BY HIS RAIN.

AND IN THAT RAIN I NEVER THOUGHT
THAT IT COULD EVER BE
THAT EVERY TIME I FAILED IT RAINED
BECAUSE GOD CRIED FOR ME.

TRACEY ROBINSON

GOD'S CREATIONS

OF ALL OF GOD'S CREATIONS,
AND ALL THE GOOD THEY'VE DONE,
DO YOU AGREE THAT MAN HAS BEEN
THE DISAPPOINTING ONE?
FROM KNOWING ONLY EDEN,
TO NOW, A WORLD AT WAR,
DID GOD, IN HIS OMNISCIENCE,
LIKE THE FUTURE WHICH HE SAW?
AND DID HE TOO FEEL SADNESS,
AS HE WATCHED THE FATE OF MAN,
WHO'S DONE HIS BEST TO SHOW HIS WORST
SINCE HIS BIRTH BEGAN?
AND WHAT OF ALL THE GOOD THINGS,
AND THE BEST OF MANKIND?
IF WE WERE EXAMINED RIGHT NOW,
WOULD THESE BE THE THINGS HE'D FIND?
THE BIRTHS OF OUR GREAT CHILDREN,
THE LOVES THAT MAN HAS SHARED.
WHEN HE LOOKS AT THE WORST OF MAN,
WILL THE BEST BE COMPARED?
GREAT LEADERS OF WORLD NATIONS

AND THOSE IN NEIGHBORHOODS,
PROTECTORS OF THE INNOCENT,
AND THOSE MISUNDERSTOOD.
THE WOMEN OF THE WORLD, I KNOW,
STAND OUT AMONG THE BEST,
FOR BOTH THE GOOD AND BAD IN MAN
MUST SEEK HER OUT TO REST.
IF I COULD SEE THE FUTURE,
I'D KNOW FATE IN ADVANCE,
FOR NOW I CAN JUST DO MY BEST
AND PRAY WE HAVE A CHANCE.

TRACEY ROBINSON

HOMELESSNESS

I SAW A SHOW ON HOMELESSNESS,
AND HOW THOSE PEOPLE LIVE,
THE PROMISES OUR COUNTRY MAKES,
THE HELP IT FAILS TO GIVE.
WE PASS THE HOMELESS EVERY DAY
AND WE AVERT OUR EYES,
FORGETTING THAT BUT FOR THE GRACE
OF GOD GO YOU OR I.
THERE ARE SOME IN SOCIETY
WHO DO NOT SEEM TO CARE
THAT THEY CANNOT PURCHASE A MEAL
OR PAY A TRANSIT FARE.
FOR SOME IT'S MENTAL ILLNESS,
SOME OTHERS CIRCUMSTANCE,
DRUG ADDICTION, PTSD,
WHILE SOME JUST NEED A CHANCE.
THE NUMBERS OF THE HOMELESS GROW
EXPONENTIALLY;
THERE ARE LOCATIONS YOU CAN GO,
WHERE THEY ARE ALL YOU SEE.
SUCH COMPLICATED ISSUES

MUST BE APPROACHED WITH CARE,
AND NOT BE MET WITH OUR DISDAIN,
OR WITH AN EMPTY STARE.
JOIN ME NOW, AT LEAST IN THOUGHT,
SO ONE DAY WE DEFEAT
THE OBSTACLES AFFECTING THOSE
WHO LIVE ON OUR MEAN STREETS.

TRACEY ROBINSON

HOW DO YOU RATE?

HOW DO YOU RATE EXISTENCE?
HOW DO YOU DEFINE WORTH?
IS IT THROUGH ITEMS THAT YOU'VE BOUGHT,
OR CHILDREN TO WHOM YOU'VE GIVEN BIRTH?
HOW IS IT THAT YOU CALCULATE
THE VALUE OF A SOUL?
IF JUDGEMENT COMES WHEN WE ALL DIE,
IS THIS TRUTH EVER TOLD?
HOW MANY STEPS ARE TAKEN
UPON THAT RUGGED PATH?
HOW MANY TIMES ARE WE ALL BLESSED
DESPITE THE DEVIL'S WRATH?
HOW MANY TIMES HAS SUNSHINE
SHONE FORTH AFTER THE RAIN?
HOW MANY TIMES SHOULD WE PREPARE
FOR WHEN IT STORMS AGAIN?
YOU LOOK INTO THE MIRROR,
AND ALL THAT YOU CAN SEE
IS WHO IT IS THAT YOU ARE NOW,
NOT WHO YOU USED TO BE.
AND SO OUR LIVES DEFINE US,

ALL THAT WHICH WE HOLD DEAR,
I AM DEFINED BY BLESSINGS THAT
ARE WHISPERED IN MY EAR.

TRACEY ROBINSON

I CRY, I CRY

I SIT AT HOME ALONE AND CRY,
AT LEAST ONE TIME A DAY.
I CRY FOR PEOPLE WHOM I'VE KNOWN,
WHO HAVE ALL PASSED AWAY.
I CRY FOR CHILDREN SUFFERING,
THEIR FACES GAUNT AND STARK,
I CRY FOR EVERY WOMAN
LYING FEARFUL IN THE DARK.
I CRY IN HAPPINESS,
FOR EVERY BLESSING I'VE RECEIVED,
I CRY FOR WORDS THAT I WRITE DOWN
BUT WHICH I DON'T CONCEIVE.
I CRY FOR LOST TOMORROWS,
AND BROKEN YESTERDAYS,
I CRY FOR EVERY ACTOR
WHO PERFORMS UPON LIFE'S STAGE.
I CRY FOR ALL WHO'VE BEEN KNOCKED DOWN
YET FOUND THE STRENGTH TO RISE,
I CRY FOR EVERY EXPOSED TRUTH
FOUND BURIED WITHIN LIES.
I CRY FOR SPIRITS' WHISPERS,

AND ALL THE THINGS THEY'VE SAID,
I CRY BECAUSE I NOW CAN HEAR
THE VOICES OF THE DEAD.
#INNERVOICES

IF I'D BEEN BORN A HERO

IF I'D BEEN BORN A HERO
I'D SAIL ACROSS THE SKIES,
WHILE SEARCHING IN THE DISTANCE
WITH TELESCOPIC EYES.
IF I'D BEEN BORN A MAESTRO,
I'D SIT DOWN AND I'D PLAY
A SYMPHONY OF ALL THERE WAS
THAT SPIRITS HAD TO SAY.
IF I WERE BORN THE NEXT DAY,
WOULD THAT HAVE CHANGED MY LIFE?
WOULD I BE HOME WITH CHILDREN,
AND A FAITHFUL, LOVING WIFE?
WOULD I HAVE BEEN AN EVIL MAN,
WHO DIED A VIOLENT DEATH?
WOULD I HAVE ASKED FORGIVENESS,
AS I TOOK MY DYING BREATH?
WHERE IS MY DOPPLEGANGER?
I'VE ASKED YOU THAT BEFORE,
BUT SINCE WE'VE GOT A MOMENT
LET'S TAKE TIME TO EXPLORE.
IS THERE A PERSON SOMEWHERE

WHO LOOKS THE SAME AS ME?
AND IF I FOCUSED,
AND I TRIED,
COULD I SENSE WHAT HE SEES?
IF HE SITS DOWN FOR DINNER,
WITH HIS WHOLE FAMILY THERE,
WOULD HE SENSE I WAS HUNGRY,
AND IF SO, WOULD HE CARE?
IF EVERY MISTAKE THAT I'VE MADE
WERE WRITTEN ONE BY ONE,
COULD I HAVE AVOIDED TROUBLE
BEFORE IT HAD BEGUN?
AND WHAT ABOUT OUR CHILDREN?
WOULD THEY TOO LOOK THE SAME,
ALTHOUGH THEY TOO LIVED FAR AWAY
AND WENT BY DIFFERENT NAMES?
I SIT HERE AND I CONTEMPLATE
HOW STRANGE THAT THINGS CAN BE,
WHEN SOMEONE,
SOMEWHERE IN THE WORLD,
LOOKS EXACTLY LIKE ME.

TRACEY ROBINSON

IF I HAD A FATHER WHO

IF I HAD A FATHER
WHO SAID,
"SON, TALK TO ME,"
I MAY NOT HAVE GROWN UP INTO
THE MAN THAT YOU NOW SEE.
IF I HAD A MOTHER
WHO SAID,
"SON, WHAT IS WRONG?"
I MIGHT NOT KNOW A CHILD'S WORST FEAR,
OR SUFFERED FOR SO LONG.
IF I HAD A TEACHER,
WHO SAID,
"YOU DON'T LOOK RIGHT,"
I MIGHT NOT HAVE CRIED,
ALL ALONE,
IN DEEPEST,
DARKEST NIGHT.
IF I HAD A SPIRIT
TO WHISPER,
"SON, YOU CAN,"
I MAY NOT HAVE,

AS JUST A CHILD,
TAKEN THE LIFE OF MAN.
FOR ALL OF THIS,
AND SO MUCH MORE,
WITH TEARFUL EYES I BOW,
YOUR WARRIOR,
SOUL FORGED IN FIRE,
THE MAN THAT I AM NOW.

TRACEY ROBINSON

JUST LIKE ME

WHAT MAKES A MAN FEEL USEFUL?
WHAT MAKES HIM WANT TO LIVE?
WHAT MAKES HIM FEEL THAT HE HAS MORE
TO RECEIVE AND TO GIVE?
WHO DOES HE BEND TO PLAY WITH,
WHEN HIS CHILDREN ARE ALL GROWN?
AND WITH WHOM DOES HE CONVERSE
WHEN HE SITS HOME ALONE?
HOW DOES A MAN FEEL PURPOSE,
WHEN ALL HE'S KNOWN IS PAIN?
AFTER EACH TIME HE'S FALLEN DOWN,
HOW DOES HE RISE AGAIN?
WHAT IS A MAN AFRAID OF,
WHEN HE HAS CONQUERED FEAR?
AND HOW CAN SPIRITS SAVE HIS LIFE,
WITH WHISPERS IN HIS EAR?
I ASK MYSELF THESE QUESTIONS,
FOR I CAN CLEARLY SEE,
THAT THERE BUT FOR THE GRACE OF GOD
GOES SOME MAN JUST LIKE ME.

LIFE'S CHALLENGES

FOR EVERYONE WHO FIGHTS A WAR
THAT RAGES EVERY DAY,
AGAINST DISEASE OR MENTAL PAIN,
ALTHOUGH THEY MAY NOT SAY.
DEPRESSION,
CANCER,
LUPUS PAIN,
A CHILD WITH SPECIAL NEEDS.
FOR EVERY LOSS THAT YOU ENDURE,
FOR EACH TIME YOU SUCCEED.
FOR EVERY TIME YOU CONCENTRATE
TO BEAR THE CHEMO'S PAIN.
FOR EVERY TIME YOU'VE BEEN KNOCKED DOWN,
AND RISEN UP AGAIN.
FOR EVERYONE WHO'S SAT IN FEAR,
AS DOCTORS READ THEIR CHART,
HOPING CANCER'S REACHED ITS END,
AND NOT ANOTHER START.
FOR EVERY ONE WHO FEELS AS THOUGH
THEY'RE STANDING ON A LEDGE,
WHO'S HOLDING ON BEFORE THEY TAKE

TRACEY ROBINSON

THAT STEP OFF OF THE EDGE.
FOR EVERYONE WHO'S RAISED THEIR ARMS
IN WELL EARNED VICTORY,
AGAINST A FOE THAT YOU AND I
WOULD HOPE TO NEVER SEE.
FOR EVERYONE WHO'S LOST THAT FIGHT,
AND MAY HAVE PASSED AWAY,
WE PRAY THAT WE WILL MEET AGAIN
WHEN WE TOO PASS ONE DAY.
FOR EVERYONE CONSIDERING
THE ENDING OF YOUR LIFE,
WHOSE ONCE CALM AND DETERMINED MIND
SEEMS OVERWHELMED WITH STRIFE.
FOR EVERY PARENT FRUSTRATED
AT WHAT A CHILD GOES THROUGH,
THE PRAYERS OF THE INSOMNIACS
GO OUT TO ALL OF YOU.
FOR EVERY INNER HERO
THAT MAKES IT'S PRESENCE KNOWN,
FOR EACH INNER DISCOVERY
THAT EACH OF YOU IS SHOWN.
THROUGH TEARFUL EYES I BOW MY HEAD,
IN HONOR AND IN PRAISE,
FOR WHO YOU ARE AND HOW YOU FIGHT,
IN MANY DIFFERENT WAYS.
FOR EVERY TIME YOU RISE AND FIGHT,

FOR EVERY TIME YOU WIN,
FOR EVERY LOSS THAT YOU ENDURE,
FOR EACH TIME YOU BEGIN
TO FACE THE CHALLENGES YOU KNOW
THAT SOME MAY NEVER SEE,
FOR EVERY TIME YOU REACH WITHIN
FOR THE BEST YOU CAN BE,
INSOMNIACS ALL PRAY FOR YOU,
ESPECIALLY ME.

TRACEY ROBINSON

MORE OR LESS

SOME PEOPLE WALK THROUGH LILY FIELDS
WHILE OTHERS WALK HOT COALS.
SOME SHIPS SAIL UPON QUIET SEAS
SOME CRASH UPON ITS SHOALS.
THE SUN SHINES DOWN ON MANY LIVES
AND IN ITS LIGHT THEY GROW
WHILE OTHERS FEEL DARKNESS AND RAIN
AND STORMS ARE ALL THEY KNOW.
THERE AREN'T MANY DIFFERENCES,
JUST MAINLY CIRCUMSTANCE.
SOMETIMES WHAT SEPARATES THE TWO
IS JUST A NEEDED CHANCE.
THE HOMELESS PERSON THAT YOU PASSED
WHILE YOU WERE WALKING HOME
AT ONE TIME HAD A FAMILY,
A HISTORY, A HOME.
HE MAY HAVE SERVED OUR COUNTRY
SO WE COULD HAVE THE RIGHT
TO LOOK DOWN AT HIM IN DISDAIN
JUST LIKE WE DID LAST NIGHT.
IT IS SO VERY EASY

TO ACT LIKE WE DON'T SEE
WHAT IS BECOMING OF THE WORLD
AND OUR SOCIETY.
IS THIS OUR EVOLUTION?
IS THIS HOW FAR WE'VE COME?
HAVE WE SOMEHOW BEEN HYPNOTIZED
FORGETTING WHERE WE'RE FROM?
I FEEL ASHAMED THAT I HAVE PLAYED
SOME PART IN WHAT IS WRONG,
IGNORING HOW SCENERY CHANGED
AND WHAT DID NOT BELONG.
I KNOW I CANNOT CHANGE THE WORLD
FOR I AM JUST ONE MAN,
BUT I CAN TRY TO CHANGE MYSELF
THE BEST WAY THAT I CAN.
AND NOW BEFORE I SIT BACK DOWN
TO EAT, AND WATCH TV,
I'LL THINK ABOUT THE HOMELESS MAN
LESS FORTUNATE THAN ME.

TRACEY ROBINSON

NOT OVER YET

SOME OF YOU LOOK AT ME AND SAY,
"HE'S OLD, AND HE'S ALONE,"
WHILE OTHERS LOOK AT ME IN AWE
FOR ALL THAT I'VE BEEN SHOWN.
SOME OF YOU LOOK AT ME AND SAY,
"HE'S WASTED MANY YEARS,"
WHILE OTHERS NOTE
I'VE BEEN A MAN
AND LEARNED TO FACE MY FEARS.
SOME OF YOU LOOK AT ME AND SAY,
"HE HASN'T GOT A WIFE,"
WHILE I SAY I'VE EXPERIENCED
TRUE LOVE WITHIN MY LIFE.
SOME OF YOU LOOK AT ME AND SAY,
"HE'S BEEN TO JAIL BEFORE."
I SAY I'M NOT THE MAN I WAS,
FOR I'VE BECOME MUCH MORE.
SOME OF YOU LOOK AT ME AND SAY,
"IT'S TOO LATE NOW FOR FAME."
I SEEK NO FORTUNE BUT I WANT
TO RE-DEFINE MY NAME.

SOME OF YOU LOOK AT ME AND SAY,
"HE'S COME A LONG, LONG WAY,"
AND IT IS YOU WHO HELPS ME RISE
TO FACE ANOTHER DAY.
SOME OF YOU LOOK AT ME AND SAY,
"MY BROTHER, AND MY FRIEND."
THIS IS MY MOTIVATION,
UPON THIS I DEPEND.
SOME OF YOU LOOK AT ME AND SAY,
"HE'S GOT NO PLACE ELSE TO GO,"
BUT THE SPIRITS TELL ME OTHERWISE
AND THAT'S ALL I NEED TO KNOW.

TRACEY ROBINSON

PRAYING FOR THE FUTURE FATE OF MAN

I WALKED ALONG THE SHORE TODAY.
MY MIND WAS LOST IN THOUGHT,
REFLECTING ON THE TRUTHS I'VE LEARNED
AND LESSONS I'VE BEEN TAUGHT.
I LOOKED TOWARD THE DISTANCE
ACROSS THE ROLLING SEA
AND WONDERED IF ANOTHER SOUL
WAS LOST IN THOUGHT LIKE ME.
HAVE I REALLY MADE AN IMPACT?
WILL I LEAVE A LEGACY?
WILL SOMEONE FIND AN ARTIFACT
ATTRIBUTED TO ME?
I LOOKED BACK AT MY FOOTSTEPS.
AT TIMES THERE ARE TWO SETS.
I'VE BEEN CARRIED BY AN ANGEL WHEN
I WALLOWED IN REGRET.
MY STRENGTH HAD LEFT MY BODY,
I'D FALLEN TO THE SAND,
WHEN SPIRITS REACHED OUT THROUGH THE VOID
AND TOOK ME BY THE HAND.

AND AFTER I HAD RESTED
AND TO ME MY GIFT WAS SHOWN,
THE ANGEL ROSE AND FLEW AWAY
AND I WALKED ON ALONE.
I STOPPED TO WATCH THE RISING
OF YET ANOTHER SUN.
I PRAYED FOR THOSE WHO WOULD NOT RISE
THE VICTIMS OF A GUN.
I PRAYED FOR THOSE WHO SUFFERED
FROM ALL FORMS OF ABUSE,
I PRAYED THAT NATIONS OF THE WORLD
WOULD SOMEHOW FORM A TRUCE.
I PRAYED FOR EVERY MONSTER'S DEATH
ALTHOUGH I KNOW IT'S TRUE,
THAT AS LONG AS GOODNESS EXISTS
EVIL MUST FLOURISH TOO.
A WAVE RISES AND ROLLS ACROSS
MY BARE FEET IN THE SAND.
I STOP AS I JUST CONTEMPLATE
THE FUTURE FATE OF MAN.

TRACEY ROBINSON

RAISING THE FATE OF MAN

IF YOU HAVE EVER FELT THE NEED
TO WRITE EXCESSIVELY,
OR HAD TO DRAW A PAINTING WHICH
ONLY YOUR MIND COULD SEE.
IF YOU HAVE SEEN A SHADOW
WHERE NONE WAS THERE BEFORE,
OR IF YOU SENSED WHAT LAY BEYOND
SOME STRANGE, UNOPENED DOOR.
IF YOU SOMEHOW HEAR VOICES
AS WHISPERS IN YOUR HEAD,
OR SOMEHOW RECEIVE MESSAGES
FROM SPIRITS OF THE DEAD.
IF YOU HAVE CERTAIN TALENTS
THAT YOU CANNOT EXPLAIN,
WHICH MAKE YOU WONDER IF PERHAPS
YOU MAY HAVE GONE INSANE.
IF YOUR EYES SOMETIMES FILL WITH TEARS
AND YOU BEGIN TO CRY
FOR REASONS UNEXPLAINED TO YOU
AND YOU ASK YOURSELF WHY.
IF YOU LOOK AT A PERSON

AND YOU CAN FEEL THEIR PAIN,
IF ON SOME BRIGHT AND SUNNY DAY
YOU SENSE THE COMING RAIN.
IF YOU CAN JUST WALK DOWN A STREET
AND TAKE A BREATH OF AIR
AND GET A SENSE THAT UP AHEAD
DANGER AWAITS YOU THERE.
IF YOU CAN SLOW YOUR MOVEMENTS,
FEELING THAT YOU GO TOO FAST,
IF YOU CAN SEE SOME FUTURE SCENE
BEFORE IT'S COME TO PASS.
THEN YOU ARE OF THE CHOSEN FEW
WHO HAVE RECEIVED "THE TOUCH,"
A GIFT FROM HIGHER POWERS THAT
EXPLAINS SO VERY MUCH.
EMBRACE YOUR HIDDEN POWERS,
FOR THEY ARE YOURS ALONE,
ALTHOUGH YOU SHARE THE UNIVERSE
WITH OTHERS WHO'VE BEEN SHOWN.
USE YOUR GIFTS MOST WISELY
HELP OTHERS WHEN YOU CAN
FOR YOU WERE MEANT TO CHANGE THE WORLD
AND RAISE THE FATE OF MAN.

TRACEY ROBINSON

REFLECTIONS OF A WOMAN

A WOMAN IS A MIRROR
REFLECTING WHO WE ARE,
THE HIDDEN TRUTHS WE TRY TO HIDE,
OUR RAW, FESTERING SCARS.
WE LOOK AT HER AND SEE OURSELVES,
FOR DOES SHE NOT EXPRESS
THE GREATEST FAILURES OF MANKIND
AS WELL AS ITS SUCCESS?
A WOMAN IS A LOVER,
SHE TAKES US TO GREAT HEIGHTS.
THE THINGS SHE MAKES US SENSE AND FEEL
ON SWEATY, MOONLIT NIGHTS.
A WOMAN IS A TEACHER
AND THROUGHOUT HISTORY,
SHE'S TAUGHT US ALL WHAT WE SHOULD DO
AND WHO WE ALL SHOULD BE.
A WOMAN IS A MESSENGER,
SHE HEARS THE SPIRIT'S WORD,
THOUGH OFTENTIMES THE TRUTH SHE SPEAKS
IS SAID, BUT LEFT UNHEARD.
A WOMAN IS A COMRADE

AND IN HER WE CONFIDE
THE TRUTH THAT NO ONE KNOWS OF US,
THE SECRETS THAT WE HIDE.
A WOMAN IS A MOTHER,
A SISTER AND A WIFE.
SHE NEVER CEASES TO AMAZE
WHEN SHE GIVES BIRTH TO LIFE.
A WOMAN IS OUR GREATEST JEWEL
AND IF YOU NEED MORE PROOF,
LOOK DEEPLY IN HER EYES AND SEE
THE VOLUMES OF HER TRUTH.

TRACEY ROBINSON

THE AMBASSADOR

I HEAR SO MANY VOICES,
ALL DIFFERENT, YET THE SAME.
I PRAY TO SEE SOME FACES SOON
AND HEAR SOMEBODY'S NAME.
WILL I HEAR FROM MY FATHER.
HOW COULD THAT EVER BE?
WILL HE SAY THAT HE'S DOING WELL
AND THAT HE'S PROUD OF ME?
WILL I HEAR FROM MY BEST FRIEND
YAHKIE ALLAH SENSEI?
WILL I SIT BY WITH TEARFUL EYES
TO HEAR WHAT HE WOULD SAY?
AND WHAT ABOUT THE PASSING SOULS
WHO DRIFT BEYOND THE GATE?
WILL I SIT BY THE FIRESIDE
WITH STORIES OF THEIR FATE?
I FEEL LIKE SOME AMBASSADOR
EXCEPT I REPRESENT
THE MANY LEAGUES OF PASSING SOULS
FROM PLACES THEY'VE BEEN SENT.

THE CHAMPIONSHIP

THE REFEREE IS COUNTING,
I HEAR IT DISTANTLY.
I KNOW THAT ONCE HE REACHES TEN
THE FIGHT IS DONE FOR ME.
"ONE!"
AS I LAY ON THE FLOOR
I LOOK OUT AT THE CROWD.
MY FRIENDS ALL CHEER,
WHILE HATERS JEER.
THE ROAR IS WILD AND LOUD.
"TWO!"
THE REFEREE LOOKS DOWN AT ME
AND SLOWLY SHAKES HIS HEAD.
HE KNOWS THAT IN THE FIGHT FOR LIFE
WE ALL WILL END UP DEAD.
"THREE!"
I HAVE JUST ROLLED OVER,
I'M NO LONGER ON MY BACK,
AND IN ITS NEUTRAL CORNER
LIFE WAITS FOR ITS ATTACK.
"FOUR!"

TRACEY ROBINSON

I'VE TAKEN HEAVY BLOWS
FROM TIME AND CIRCUMSTANCE,
BUT IF I MAKE IT TO MY FEET
I MAY STILL HAVE A CHANCE.
"FIVE!"
THE WHOLE CROWD NOW IS ON ITS FEET
AS I RISE TO ONE KNEE.
I LOOK OVER AT RINGSIDE WHERE
DEATH SMILES AND WAVES AT ME.
"SIX!"
I REACH UP FOR THE HIGHEST ROPE
AND PULL WITH ALL MY STRENGTH.
I HAVE TO MAKE IT TO MY FEET
AND FIGHT LIFE TO ITS LENGTH.
FOR YEARS I'VE TAKEN COMBOS,
THE BEST THAT LIFE COULD THROW,
WHILE DEATH STALKED FRIENDS AND RELATIVES
AND PEOPLE THAT I KNOW.
I'VE STRUCK BACK WITH MY BLESSINGS,
LIKE CHILDREN AND GOOD HEALTH.
I'VE LIVED THROUGH TIMES OF POVERTY
AND SEEN SOME FORMS OF WEALTH.
I'VE HAD MY SHARE OF FREEDOM,
I'VE LIVED WITHIN A CELL,
AND I'VE HEARD SPIRITS' VOICES THAT
I'VE COME TO KNOW SO WELL.

"SEVEN!"
YELLED THE REFEREE
AS I BEGAN TO STAND.
HE DIDN'T TRY TO HELP ME BUT
HE HAD TO TAKE MY HAND.
I TOOK A GLANCE AT LIFE AND SAW
THAT HE WAS QUITE SURPRISED,
WHEN HE SAW THE DETERMINED LOOK
THAT FELL ACROSS MY EYES.
I FELT WHATEVER STRENGTH I HAD
WAS DRAWING INTO PLAY
FOR I DECIDED IN MY HEART
I WOULD NOT DIE TODAY!
"EIGHT!"
SCREAMED THE REFEREE
AND SIGNALLED US TO FIGHT.
I RAN ACROSS THE RING TO LIFE
SWINGING BOTH LEFTS AND RIGHTS!
I PUMMELED LIFE WITH ALL I HAD.
HE STUMBLED TWO STEPS BACK,
AND AS HE FELL AGAINST THE ROPES
I CONTINUED MY ATTACK.
AND AS WE CLINCHED I SPOKE TO HIM,
I TOLD LIFE OF MY PLANS
TO PUBLISH ALL MY WRITINGS AND
TO HELP MY FELLOW MAN.

TRACEY ROBINSON

I TOOK TWO STEPS BACK AND SWUNG HARD,
TWO LEFT BLOWS AND A RIGHT,
AND LIFE WENT DOWN TO JUST ONE KNEE,
FIRST TIME EVER IN A FIGHT.
LIFE ROSE BACK UP QUICKLY
AND I BACKED UP AS WELL.
IT SEEMS WE BOTH HAD ROUNDS TO GO
AND STORIES LEFT TO TELL.
I TOOK HOME THE DECISION,
CHAMPION FOR A DAY,
BUT IN THIS FIGHT OF LIFE AND DEATH
FATE CAN GO EITHER WAY.
I SAW DEATH LEAVING, QUITE DISTURBED
HE'D LOST ANOTHER BET.
WE BOTH KNEW WE WOULD MEET AGAIN,
BUT NOT TODAY, NOT YET.
AFTER THE FIGHT, LIFE AND I HUGGED,
AND TO MY GREAT SURPRISE
HE LOOKED AT ME AND NODDED
THROUGH SWEATY, TEAR-STAINED EYES.
"YOU'VE BEEN A GREAT OPPONENT,
THE BEST I'VE SEEN SO FAR!
KEEP UP THOSE HANDS,
PROTECT YOUR FACE,
AND STAY JUST WHO YOU ARE!"
HE TURNED JUST THEN AND WALKED AWAY,

HIS ENTOURAGE IN TOW.
I WAVED AT FRIENDS AND FAMILY
ALL THOSE I LOVE AND KNOW.

THE DAWNING OF THIS DAY

I'VE SEEN THE DAWNING OF THIS DAY
AND WONDERED WHAT IT BRINGS.
A SQUIRREL JUST SCAMPERED QUICKLY BY,
SOMEWHERE A CAGED BIRD SINGS.
THE SKIES ARE SLOWLY DARKENING,
IT SEEMS ABOUT TO RAIN.
DOES THIS MEAN THAT THE DAY WOULD BRING
BAD CIRCUMSTANCE OR PAIN?
IS MOTHER EARTH ABOUT TO CRY
FOR WHAT THIS DAY WILL HOLD?
AND WHAT APOCALYPTIC FATE
MUST ALL MANKIND BEHOLD?
AND WHAT IF ALL THE CLOUDS CLEAR UP
AND SUNSHINE BLAZES THROUGH,
WILL THAT ALTER THE FUTURE WHICH
THE RAIN WOULD PUT US THROUGH?
AND IF IT BECOMES WINDY
WILL BREEZES BLOW AWAY
THE HOPE AND DREAMS THAT WE HOLD DEAR,
THE WORDS WE DO NOT SAY?
DO SNOWY DAYS JUST BLIND US

SO THAT WE CANNOT SEE
THAT SOME RELATIONSHIPS WE START
ARE NEVER MEANT TO BE?
IF WEATHER COULD CONTROL US
THEN ALL OF US WOULD FAIL,
LIKE A SHIP WITHOUT A RUDDER WE
WOULD HAVE NO WAY TO SAIL.
I'VE SEEN THE DAWNING OF THIS DAY
AND AS I SLOWLY RISE
THE SPIRITS WHISPER IN MY EARS
AND TRUTH IS IN MY EYES.

TRACEY ROBINSON

THE DESTINY YOU CHOOSE

THE DEVIL VISITS QUIETLY,
THE BURGLAR IN YOUR LIFE.
HE DOESN'T WAKE THE CHILDREN OR
YOUR SOUNDLY SLEEPING WIFE.
HE ASKS YOU SOFTLY IN YOUR EAR,
"WHAT SHALL WE DO TODAY?"
THERE'S NO NEED FOR YOU TO RESPOND,
HE KNOWS JUST WHAT YOU'LL SAY.
THE DEVIL SMILES DOWN AT YOUR WIFE
AND CARESSES HER ASS.
SHE SIGHS AND MOVES CLOSER TO YOU
WHILE YOU THINK OF SINS PAST.
FOR THOSE OF YOU WITH HUSBANDS.
THE DEVIL LOOKS AT YOU.
AND SMILES AT ALL THE SECRETS
KEPT JUST BETWEEN YOU TWO.
WE ALL WAKE UP AND TRY TO CHANGE
SOME SMALL THINGS AND SOME BIG,
A DAILY PROMISE THAT WE MAKE
ON WHICH SOMETIMES WE RENEGE.
WE DIG DEEPLY WITHIN US,

WE OFTEN OVERCOME.
THE DEVIL LOOKS IN ANGERED AWE
AT WHERE OUR STRENGTH COMES FROM.
AN ANGEL HOVERS QUIETLY
AND WATCHES AS YOU SLEEP
WHILE SPIRITS WHISPER IN YOUR MIND
EXPANDING THOUGHTS SO DEEP.
IT KNOWS YOUR ASPIRATIONS,
IT HAS SEEN ALL YOUR GOALS.
IT'S SEEN THE WAVES OF SADNESS THAT
HAVE CRASHED UPON YOUR SHOALS.
IT KNOWS THE DEVIL IS WITH YOU,
IT WATCHES AS YOU CHOOSE.
THE SPIRITS DANCE AS ONCE AGAIN
THE DEVIL LEARNS TO LOSE.
YOU WILL NOT SMOKE THAT CIGARETTE,
YOU WILL NOT TAKE THAT DRINK.
YOU WILL GO OUT AND CHASE YOUR DREAMS—
WHO CARES WHAT PEOPLE THINK?
YOU WILL OVERCOME OBSTACLES,
YOU WILL NOT STEAL OR LIE.
YOU'LL HUG YOUR CHILDREN WHILE THEY LAUGH
AND HOLD THEM WHEN THEY CRY.
YOU'LL BE THE BEST THAT YOU CAN BE
AND SEEING THIS WILL SHOW
THE DEVIL THAT HE'S FAILED TODAY

TRACEY ROBINSON

AND IT WAS TIME TO GO.
THE DEVIL BURST FORTH FROM YOUR HOME
IN SILENCE, BUT ON FIRE.
THE ANGEL FLOATS MAJESTICALLY.
ITS LOOK IS PROUD, YET DIRE.
THERE IS NO NEED FOR THEM TO SPEAK,
IT'S ALL BEEN SAID BEFORE.
THE DEVIL'S HAD SOME VICTORIES,
HE LEAVES IN SEARCH OF MORE.
THE ANGEL FLIES OFF ALSO,
WITH MANY DEEDS TO DO.
SO MANY DESTINIES TO CHOOSE
BEFORE OUR LIVES ARE THROUGH.

THE EVIL SPIRITS 'LURKING'

A VERY EVIL SPIRIT
DROVE QUIETLY ONE NIGHT.
HE LOOKED JUST LIKE AN AVERAGE MAN,
HIS BUILD WAS SHORT AND SLIGHT.
HE'D ROAMED THE EARTH FOR MANY YEARS,
FAR MORE THAN HE COULD COUNT,
AND HE'D DESTROYED THOUSANDS OF LIVES—
WHO KNEW THE TRUE AMOUNT?
"WHOSE LIFE SHOULD I RUIN TODAY?"
THE EVIL SPIRIT SAID.
"WHOSE FUTURE SHOULD I DEVASTATE
OR SHOULD I KILL INSTEAD?"
HE THOUGHT OF SOME SCENARIOS
AND POSSIBILITIES
AS HIS EYES SCANNED THE CITY STREETS
TO SEE WHOM HE COULD SEE.
"SHOULD I MAKE SOMEONE TAKE A DRINK
AND WASH AWAY THEIR SOUL?
JUST SQUEEZE THAT WARMLY BEATING HEART
UNTIL IT'S STIFF AND COLD?
OR MAKE THAT YOUNG GIRL RUN AWAY

TRACEY ROBINSON

THINKING THAT SHE'LL DANCE,
THEN SEVERAL YEARS FROM NOW SHE'LL SEE
SHE NEVER HAD A CHANCE?
MAYBE I'LL GIVE THAT YOUNG MAN
A HIT OF CRACK COCAINE.
HE WON'T KNOW HOW IT STARTED AND
HE WON'T KNOW WHOM TO BLAME.
I'LL TAKE AWAY SOME CHILDREN'S DREAMS
AND ROB THEM OF THEIR GOALS.
THEIR LIVES WILL SOON COME CRASHING DOWN.
LIKE WAVES UPON THE SHOALS!"
THE SPIRIT FELT QUITE FINE IT SEEMED,
LIKE EVERY OTHER NIGHT,
UNTIL HE HEARD THE SIRENS AND
HE SAW THE FLASHING LIGHTS.
"SHIT!" THE SPIRIT SAID OUT LOUD
"PRAYER WARRIOR PATROL!"
A SHIVER SLID RIGHT DOWN HIS SPINE,
HE SUDDENLY FELT COLD.
HE PULLED HIS CAR RIGHT OVER
AND AS HE GLANCED ABOUT
HE LOOKED AND SAW THAT FROM THEIR CAR
PRAYER WARRIORS GOT OUT.
IT WASN'T JUST A CAR, HE SAW,
IT LOOKED MORE LIKE A TRUCK,
AND BOTH THE WARRIORS LOOKED BIG,

THEIR WINGS WERE NEATLY TUCKED.
THEY TOOK HIS INFORMATION
AND ONE WENT BACK TO CHECK.
HE FELT THE OTHER'S EYES ON HIM
LIKE HEAT UPON HIS NECK.
AFTER AWHILE THE ONE RETURNED
AND THEY SAID TO GET OUT.
THE SPIRIT QUIETLY COMPLIED—
IT MADE NO SENSE TO SHOUT.
THE WARRIORS HAD ONLY SAID,
"WE KNOW JUST WHO YOU ARE,"
AS THEY JUST SHUFFLED HIM ALONG
AND THREW HIM IN THEIR CAR.
IT SEEMED THAT HE HAD WARRANTS
FOR EVIL DONE BEFORE;
THE WARRIORS CAUGHT UP WITH HIM
BEFORE HE COULD DO MORE.
THE PEOPLE ON THE STREET COULD NOT
SEE ANY OF THESE THINGS,
SO FEW CAN SEE THE SPIRITS OR
THE GOOD AND BAD THEY BRING.

TRACEY ROBINSON

THE JUNGLE

JUST LIKE WE SEE IN NATURE
WE SEE IN MAN EACH DAY:
WHILE SOME MEN LIVE AS PREDATORS,
SOME OTHERS FALL AS PREY.
LIKE ANY OTHER JUNGLE,
THE CITY HAS ALL BREEDS.
SO MANY PEOPLE CO-EXIST
AND SATISFY THEIR NEEDS.
SOME CHILDREN THAT ARE RAISED WILL RISE
LIKE BIRDS ACROSS THE SKY,
WHILE OTHERS BECOME SCAVENGERS
AND NONE OF US KNOW WHY.
AND LIKE A JUNGLE, THERE ARE BEASTS
WITH NO KNOWN THREAT BUT MAN.
WE ALL STAY ARMED AND VILIGANT
TO SURVIVE AS BEST WE CAN.
THE JUNGLE HAS GORILLAS,
THE CITY HAS THEM TOO.
THEY PREY UPON THE OLD AND WEAK
AND ARE NO THREAT TO YOU.
SOME PEOPLE HAVE THE STRANGEST WAYS

AND UNDERHANDED STYLES,
REMINDING US OF MONKEYS OR
SOME FORM OF SLY REPTILE.
THE CITY'S BARS ARE WATER HOLES.
LIKE ANIMALS WE DRINK,
AND TO THE DEPTHS OF WATER HOLES
LIKE ANIMALS WE SINK.
LIONS GATHER ON THE PLAINS
TO HUNT AND SEE WHAT YIELDS,
WHILE CITY SCHOOLS HAVE NOW BECOME
LIKE JUNGLE KILLING FIELDS.
MALE LIONS SEEMED THE KING OF BEASTS,
UNTIL WE WATCHED TO LEARN,
THE LIONESS DID ALL THE WORK
FOR FOOD HE NEVER EARNED.
WE HAVE OUR WOMEN HERE AS WELL
WHO BEAR MOST OF THE WEIGHT,
WHEN DEALING WITH A MAN WITH NO
CONCERN OF CHILDREN'S FATE.
THE CITY HAS ITS WARRIORS,
STRONG MEN LIKE FROM OUR PAST,
ON WHOM YOU CAN DEPEND,
WHO'S LOVE WILL ALWAYS LAST.
THE JUNGLE HAS ITS ANIMALS
THAT STALK DURING THE NIGHT;
THE CITY HAS ITS MONSTERS THAT

TRACEY ROBINSON

PREY ON THE YOUNG AND SLIGHT.
AS WISE ONES WE MUST BE ALL KINDS
AND ACT AS EVERY BREED,
DEPENDING ON THE CIRCUMSTANCE
OR PARTICULAR NEED.
YOU MAY FIGHT LIKE A LION,
READY TO RIP AND SLAY.
YOU MAY RUN LIKE A CHEETAH
TO FIGHT ANOTHER DAY.
YOU MAY BE LIKE AN OWL
TO FIGURE OUT A PLAN
TO RISE ABOVE ADVERSITY
AND SURVIVE AS BEST YOU CAN.
LIKE SOME GIGANTIC GRIZZLY BEAR
WE ALL PROTECT OUR YOUNG.
LIKE ELEPHANTS WE DON'T FORGET
JUST WHERE IT IS WE'RE FROM.
THE WORLD IS STILL OUR PARADISE
IF WE TREAT IT AS SUCH.
THE JUNGLE HOLDS ITS MYSTERIES
AND WE CAN ALL LEARN MUCH.

THE LAUNDRY ROOM

SITTING
DOING LAUNDRY,
AND IT OCCURED TO ME,
THE WAY WE LIVE OUR LIVES IS LIKE
THE VERY THINGS I SEE.
FOR DO WE NOT GET SOILED IN LIFE
BECAUSE WE TOIL EACH DAY?
AND DO WE NOT ALL TAKE THE TIME
TO WASH THAT SOIL AWAY?
THE SOIL OF DISAPPOINTMENT,
SOMETIMES THE SOIL OF PAIN,
THE SOIL OF HAVING TO DEAL WITH
SOME PEOPLE YOU DISDAIN.
OUR DRYERS ARE VACATIONS,
WHERE WE SIT IN THE SUN.
WE FRESHEN UP AND WE RELAX
UNTIL WE FEEL UNSPUN.
OUR CLOTHES ARE SEPARATED
LIKE ASPECTS OF LIFE'S DAYS.
OUR FRIENDS ARE CHARACTERIZED BY
OUR TASTES, PLEASURES AND WAYS.

TRACEY ROBINSON

AND ONCE WE'RE CLEAN,
WE'RE BACK ON DECK,
FORGETFUL OF THE GLOOM.
THE WAY I'LL FEEL WHEN I PACK UP
AND LEAVE THIS LAUNDRY ROOM.

THE LIFE

THE LIFE THAT I NOW LIVE TODAY
IS NOT LIKE LIFE BEFORE.
I NOW SEE SPIRITS IN THE AIR,
HEAR VOICES
AND MUCH MORE.
THEY CIRCLE ALL AROUND ME,
THEY PEEK INSIDE MY HEAD.
THEY TAKE THEIR NOTES,
AND GIVE THEIR QUOTES,
AND I WRITE WHAT THEY SAID.
FOR MANY YEARS THEY'VE TALKED TO ME,
SINCE I WAS VERY YOUNG.
I THOUGHT IT WAS MY CONSCIENCE
OR JUST SONGS LEFT UNSUNG.
SOMETIMES WHEN I JUST LONG FOR SLEEP
THEY WAKE ME UP TO LOOK
WHILE I, WITH NOTHING ELSE TO DO,
JUST STAY UP LATE TO COOK.
THEY KNOW THEY CANNOT TASTE IT,
COULD THEY EVEN SMELL MY FOOD?
DOES IT BRING BACK THEIR MEMORIES

TRACEY ROBINSON

OR HELP IMPROVE THEIR MOODS?
I'VE FELT THE REAPER'S COLD HOT KISS,
MY LIFE HAS TASTED DEATH.
I'VE SAT IN SILENCE MANY TIMES
AS FRIENDS TOOK THEIR LAST BREATH.
I THINK THAT WHEN I MAKE THOSE MEALS
I REALLY HOPE ONE DAY
THAT SOME GOOD FRIEND WOULD VISIT ME
AND WOULD DECIDE TO STAY.
MY SOLITUDE, MY ARMOR,
I WEAR IT LIKE A VEST
A BROKEN BUT RECOVERING HEART
BEATS STRONGLY IN MY CHEST.
I FEEL MY WORLD IS SHRINKING;
I SLOWLY SINK WITHIN
THE QUICKSAND OF REALITY,
THE ATONEMENT OF SIN.
THE DEEPER THAT I'M DRAWN WITHIN
THE MORE I TRY TO FIND,
IF I'M A MAN THAT HAS BEEN BLESSED
OR ONE WHO'S LOST HIS MIND?

THE MAP OF LIFE

A WOMAN'S BODY IS A MAP
WITH DETAILS OF HER LIFE.
JUST SIT AND STUDY ALL THE SKIN
OF YOUR GIRLFRIEND OR WIFE.
HER STRETCH MARKS ARE TRIBUTARIES
WHICH BLEND AND FORM AS ONE.
EACH HOLDS CERTAIN MEMORIES
OF HOW LIFE HAD BEGUN.
TRACE THE LINES WITH MUCH RESPECT
FOR SHE'S FELT PAIN FOR YOU.
CHERISH ALL THAT YOUR QUEEN IS
AND ALL THAT YOU'VE BEEN THROUGH.
BEAUTY MAY LAST FOREVER
IF ONLY FROM THE HEART,
FOR DID YOUR SOULS NOT TAKE ROOT FIRST
RIGHT FROM THE VERY START?
THE SCAR FROM HER C-SECTION
YOU'VE NOT SEEN IN A WHILE,
LET US LABEL ON THE MAP
THAT AS THE RIVER NILE.
FOR HAVE YOU NOT BOTH TAKEN SAIL,

TRACEY ROBINSON

HAVE YOU NOT LIVED GOOD YEARS?
HAVE YOU NOT TIPPED THE SCALES TOWARD "GOOD,"
REGARDLESS OF THE TEARS?
SOME OF YOU MAY ALSO SEE
SOME SCARS THAT YOU LEFT THERE,
WHEN YOU LASHED OUT IN ANGER
THAT YOU KNEW WAS NOT FAIR.
YOU MAY HAVE BEEN FORGIVEN,
OR PERHAPS YOU WERE NOT,
BUT THE MEMORY OF THAT DAY
IS NOT ONE YOU FORGOT.
LOOK AT HOW HER LAUGH LINES CHANGED,
IN ALL THE YEARS GONE BY.
HER TEARS HAVE TRACED THOSE LAUGHING LINES
WITH EACH TIME THAT SHE'S CRIED.
NOW THAT YOU'VE SEEN THE MAP OF LIFE
JUST STAND AND TAKE A BOW,
FOR QUEENS WHO EXCEL ALL THROUGH LIFE
AND NEVER TELL US HOW.

THE MESMERIST

I AM THE MENTAL MESMERIST.
I STAND UPON MY STAGE,
SURROUNDED BY AN AUDIENCE,
ALL GENDERS, RACES, AND AGES.
MY GIFT IS THAT I SEE INSIDE
OF OTHER PEOPLE'S MINDS.
I LOOK AT YOU, I SEE YOUR THOUGHTS,
AND TELL YOU WHAT I FIND.
LIKE YOU, YOUNG LADY SITTING THERE,
SO ELOQUENTLY DRESSED,
NO ONE ELSE COULD EVER SEE
THAT YOUR LIFE IS A MESS.
IT SEEMS THAT TROUBLE FOLLOWS YOU,
ESPECIALLY IN MEN.
YOU PROMISED THAT IT NEVER WOULD,
BUT IT'S HAPPENED ONCE AGAIN.
HE JUST DOES NOT RESPECT YOU,
HE DOES NOT SHARE YOUR DREAMS.
HE DRANK AND CURSED THE OTHER NIGHT,
AND YOU KNOW WHAT THAT MEANS.
BUT HAVE NO FEAR, YOUNG LADY,

TRACEY ROBINSON

FOR THINGS WILL NOW SOON CHANGE.
I SEE DECISIONS THAT YOU MAKE,
I SEE FATE RE-ARRANGED!
I SEE YOU FIRST COMPLETING SCHOOL,
I SEE YOU WORKING HARD,
I SEE THAT ALL WHO KNOW YOU STILL
HOLD YOU IN HIGH REGARD.
I SEE YOU RISING GREATLY,
I SEE YOUR DUE SUCCESS,
I WISH YOU YEARS OF BETTER DAYS
AND I SEE YOUR HAPPINESS.
AND YOU, MY FRIEND, ARE WORRIED
ABOUT YOUR SOLDIER SON,
IF HE WILL LIVE, SINCE NOW IT SEEMS
ANOTHER WAR'S BEGUN.
REACH UP TO ME MY BROTHER,
I MUST EXTEND MY TOUCH.
THIS VISION THAT I SEEK TO SEE
I CANNOT MISS BY MUCH.
MY GOD, I SEE SUCH BLOODSHED,
I SEE MUCH DEATH AND PAIN.
SO MANY SOULS SHALL RISE UP WHEN
THE WORLD CRIES CRIMSON RAIN.
BUT THROUGH IT ALL
YOUR SON SHALL LIVE,
ROBERTO IS HIS NAME.

BUT YOUR BELOVED ROBERTO
HE WILL NOT BE THE SAME.
HE WILL HAVE WITNESSED FRIENDS EXPLODE
FROM HIDDEN IED'S.
HE'LL CARRY GUILT AND ASK HIMSELF,
"WHY COULD IT NOT BE ME?!"
HE WILL HAVE TASTED HUMAN BLOOD
AS VAPOR IN THE AIR;
HE'LL SEE PEOPLE WHO DISAPPEARED
WHERE ONCE THEY STOOD RIGHT THERE.
SO BE PREPARED
TO SHOW SUPPORT
IN EVERY WAY YOU CAN
YOUR SON LIES SOMEWHERE DEEP INSIDE
THAT RETURNING YOUNG MAN.
YOU THERE, MOTHER,
DON'T YOU BE TOO UPSET:
YOUR DAUGHTER WILL SOON GET YOUR POINT
SHE JUST DOESN'T SEE IT YET.
WAIT! YOU, SIR, ARE A MONSTER!
WHAT ARE YOU DOING HERE?!
DID YOU NOT THINK THAT I WOULD SENSE
IF YOU WERE TO COME NEAR?!
LOOK CLOSELY, MY DEAR AUDIENCE!
FOR THIS IS HOW THEY LOOK.
THEY'LL PASS BY WITHOUT NOTICE

TRACEY ROBINSON

IN JUST THE TIME IT TOOK.
SINCE YOU'RE HERE I'LL READ TO SEE
WHAT KIND OF BEAST YOU ARE.
TO WHAT PERVERSION DO YOU LEAN?
WHAT'S YOUR PROCLIVITY?
AHHH, YOU LIKE THE CHILDREN,
YOU WICKED LITTLE BEAST!
THE ONES WHO SEEM THE EASIEST,
THE ONES WHO FIGHT THE LEAST!
I SEE YOUR FUTURE CLEARLY;
WOULD YOU TOO LIKE TO SEE?
HEY! WAIT! WHY DO YOU LEAVE?
DON'T RUN AWAY FROM ME!
I GUESS THAT IS ENOUGH FOR NOW,
HOW ABOUT A LITTLE BREAK?
THAT LAST READING WAS STRESSFUL
AND A LITTLE HARD TO TAKE.
LET'S HAVE A QUIET INTERLUDE
AND THEN BEGIN AGAIN.
AND WHEN WE DO, I'LL START WITH YOU,
MY YOUNGER, NERVOUS FRIEND.

THE MURDER OF...

I'VE TAKEN AS MUCH TIME AS I COULD
AS I TRIED TO AVOID
THE FEELINGS THAT I HAVE OVER
THE MURDER OF GEORGE FLOYD.
"I CAN'T BREATHE!
I CAN'T BREATHE!
I CAN'T BREATHE!"
THIS IS NOT A CHANT I SHOUT,
IT IS NOT SOME HOT NEW SONG.
THOSE WORDS WERE UTTERED
ON TWO TIMES
LAW ENFORCEMENT WENT WRONG.
MR. ERIC GARNER.
ALTHOUGH WE'D NEVER MET.
THE CIRCUMSTANCES OF YOUR DEATH
THE WORLD WILL NOT FORGET.
AT LEAST THAT'S WHAT I FELT UNTIL
THE MURDER OF GEORGE FLOYD
NOW LIFE HAS CHANGED
FROM EVERYTHING
WE'D PREVIOUSLY ENJOYED.

TRACEY ROBINSON

YOU'D THINK THAT COPS KNEW BETTER.
WITH BODY CAMS AND ALL,
BUT SUNS RISE UP
AND THEN THEY SET,
WHICH IS TO SAY,
THEY FALL.
WE LOOK TOWARD THE HORIZON,
BUT IT IS NOT THE SAME.
THE NIGHT'S ALIVE WITH PROTESTS
AND THE NIGHT'S ALIGHT WITH FLAME.
THE TRUST HAS BEEN ALL BROKEN,
BOUNDARIES NO LONGER CLEAR.
WHERE CITIZENS ONCE HAD CONFIDENCE
SOME NOW ONLY FEEL FEAR.
AND THEN THERE ARE THE ANGRY,
A MULTITUDE OF ONE,
WHO'VE SET THE TONE
AND RAISED THEIR CRIES,
NO ACTIONS BEEN UNDONE.
I'VE SAT IN MEDITATION,
I'VE CLOSED MY EYES IN PRAYER,
I'VE EVEN ASKED THE SPIRITS,
BUT IT SEEMS THEY WEREN'T THERE.
THE SPIRITS HAVEN'T LEFT ME, THOUGH,
I FEEL THEM BY MY SIDE.
THEIR SILENCE MAY SHOW THEIR RESPECTS

FOR ERIC FLOYD'S LAST RIDE.
WE WON'T GO OUT AND RIOT,
INSOMNIACS DON'T LOOT.
BUT FOR OUR FALLEN BROTHERS WE
SHALL STAND UP AND SALUTE!
THE LIFE YOU'VE LIVED, YOUR FAMILIES,
AND ALL YOU LOVED THE MOST,
SHALL BE FOREVER IN OUR PRAYERS
AS WE RAISE OUR DRINKS IN TOAST.
EINSTEIN SAID TO REPEAT THINGS
YET EXPECT DIFFERENT ENDS
DEFINES THE WORD "INSANITY,"
AND HE WAS RIGHT
MY FRIENDS.
I DID NOT WRITE TO UPSET THOSE
ALREADY UP ON EDGE.
I HOPE IN FACT I WRITE TO THOSE
WHO HOLD THAT LINE,
STANDING OUT ON THAT LEDGE.
BELOW US LIES A DARK ABYSS
AND ITS CALLED ANARCHY.
THE THINGS WE WATCH NOW
ON THE NEWS
IS HOW OUR WORLD WILL BE.
SO
WHO'LL PROTECT THE PUBLIC

TRACEY ROBINSON

FROM CRIMES
AND WHAT CROOKS DO?
THE GOOD POLICE
WHO SERVE WITH PRIDE,
AND THERE ARE QUITE A FEW.
AS YOU MEASURE JUSTICE
ON SCALES WITHIN YOUR MIND,
BE OBJECTIVE,
FOR THE TRUTH
IS THERE FOR YOU TO FIND.

THE 'PHILOSOPHICAL' QUESTION

A TREE FALLS IN THE FOREST
BUT NO ONE IS AROUND,
SO WILL THE TREE FALL QUIETLY
WITHOUT MAKING A SOUND?
IF ALL THE WORLD WAS JUST A STAGE
AND ON IT OUR LIVES PLAYED,
COULD I HAVE ASKED FOR A SCRIPT CHANGE
AND HAD MY FATE DELAYED?
COULD I HAVE PLAYED A DIFFERENT ROLE
AND NEVER GONE TO JAIL?
WOULD I HAVE LEARNED HOW TO SUCCEED
INSTEAD OF HOW TO FAIL?
BACK INSIDE THE FOREST,
THE PREDATOR SEEKS PREY.
WHEN FIRE STRIKES THEY UNIFY
AS THEY ALL RUN AWAY.
I THOUGHT I HEARD A CRY OUTSIDE,
ANOTHER CHILD IS BORN.
ANOTHER CRY, ANOTHER PLACE
WHERE SOME HEART IS FORLORN.

TRACEY ROBINSON

WE ALL GET PHILOSOPHICAL
WHEN IT IS TIME TO DIE,
AND ALL WE REALLY WANT TO SAY
IS, "NO GOD, NOT ME. PLEASE, WHY?"

THE PLACE WHERE BLUE WHALES GO TO DIE

PART ONE

I TRAVELED TO A PLACE LAST NIGHT
WITH DEATH RIGHT BY MY SIDE.
HE CAME TO VISIT AS I SLEPT
AND SAID, "LET'S TAKE A RIDE."
I'D LIKE TO SHOW YOU BRIEFLY
SOME OF THE THINGS I SEE,
AND ALSO TO PROVIDE YOU WITH
MORE INSIGHT INTO ME.
AND SO IT WAS I FELT THAT I
BEGAN TO RISE AND FLY.
DEATH SAID THE PLACE WE SEEK IS WHERE
HORIZON MEETS THE SKY.
WE PASSED OVER A CITY
THAT BLAZED WITH FLASHING LIGHTS.
LIKE FIREWORKS THEY GLITTERED
EXPLODING IN THE NIGHT.
"EACH FLASH YOU SEE BELOW,"
DEATH SAID,
"MEANS ONE MORE LIFE WAS LOST.

TRACEY ROBINSON

BUT HUMANS ONLY MEASURE DEATH
BY WHAT TO THEM IT COSTS.
BUT WITHOUT DEATH THERE IS NO LIFE,
A CIRCLE, YING AND YANG.
JOY AND PAIN BOTH TAUGHT YOU WHY
A BIRD THOUGH CAGED STILL SANG.
WHAT PEOPLE CALL NOURISHMENT,
VEGAN OR OMNIVORE,
REPRESENTS DEATH ON SUCH A SCALE
I GAVE UP KEEPING SCORE!
OCEANS DEPLETED OF THEIR FISH,
TREES ROBBED OF PRECIOUS FRUIT,
ANIMALS SLAUGHTERED AIMLESSLY,
PLANTS RIPPED UP BY THEIR ROOTS.
YOU GIVE KIDS CANDY KISSES,
FROM KILLED COCA THEY CAME,
AND FROM THOSE VERY COCA LEAVES
MAN PROCESSES COCAINE.
BUT LOOK NOW, DOWN BELOW YOU,
SEE A DIFFERENT LIGHT.
FOR THERE YOU'LL SEE EACH CHILD WHO'S BORN
THROUGHOUT THE WORLD AT NIGHT."
I LOOKED DOWN AND I SAW THEM.
THEY TWINKLED SOFT AND GOLD.
I SAW A TRUTH GREATER THAN ANY
STORY I'D BEEN TOLD.

"I'VE HAD SEVERAL RELATIONSHIPS,"
DEATH SAID TO ME JUST THEN,
"AND I'VE HAD MEN AND WOMEN WHOM
I CAME TO CALL MY FRIENDS.
BUT ALL I FELT WAS SORROW
FOR ALWAYS CAME THE DAY
WHEN EVERYONE I KNEW WOULD DIE
AND DEATH TAKES THEM AWAY."
I THOUGHT I SAW DEATH CRY JUST THEN,
BUT IT HAD STARTED TO RAIN.
DEATH MAY NOT HAVE SHED A TEAR
BUT I STILL FELT HIS PAIN.
AFTER A WHILE OF FLYING
WE FINALLY CAME TO REST;
I COULD NOT QUITE CONCEAL MY AWE,
ALTHOUGH I DID MY BEST.
WE WERE ATOP THE WORLD
IT SEEMED, AND THERE,
IN FRONT OF ME,
GIANT BLUE WHALES SHONE WITH LIGHT
AND LEAPT UP OUT THE SEA.
WE HEARD A HAUNTING MELODY,
WE WATCHED THE LEAPING WHALES,
UNTIL THEIR LEAPING BECAME LESS
AND THEN THEIR EFFORTS FAILED.
THE GATHERING OF WHALES STILL SANG

TRACEY ROBINSON

A SAD SONG OF FAREWELL.
I WONDERED WHAT THEY ALL HAD SEEN,
THE STORIES THEY COULD TELL.
AFTER A WHILE THE SEA CALMED DOWN,
BLUE LIGHTS NO LONGER SHONE,
AND THAT LEFT ONLY DEATH AND I
AS WE BOTH SAT ALONE.
THIS IS THE PLACE I SPOKE OF,
WHERE HORIZON MEETS THE SKY.
FOR THIS IS WHERE THE BLUE WHALES COME
WHEN IT'S TIME FOR THEM TO DIE.
BLUE WHALES HAVE NO PREDATORS,
SO THEY LIVE TRULY FREE.
THEY DO NOT HAVE TO KILL FOR FOOD,
THEY DON'T KNOW SAVAGERY.
THE LARGEST CREATURES IN THE SEA,
THEY SWAM THE OCEAN'S DEPTHS.
THE HISTORY THAT THEY HAVE SEEN,
THE SECRETS THEY HAVE KEPT.
"I THANK YOU FRIEND FOR COMING,"
DEATH TURNED TO ME AND SAID.
I FELL ASLEEP, AND WHEN I WOKE,
I WAS BACK IN MY BED.

THE PLACE WHERE BLUE WHALES GO TO DIE

PART TWO

{A CONVERSATION WITH DEATH}

I THOUGHT THAT I'D SLEPT SOUNDLY
SO I DID NOT KNOW WHY
I OPENED UP MY EYES AND SAW
A MOON
AND STARLIT SKY.
I LOOKED AROUND CURIOUSLY,
AND CAUTIOUSLY AS WELL:
SINCE I RECENTLY KILLED DEATH'S SON
I THOUGHT THIS MIGHT BE HELL.
I SAT UP,
SAW THAT I WAS DRESSED,
THEN I PREPARED TO STAND,
WHEN I NOTICED THE SPIRIT'S BLADE
HELD FIRMLY IN MY HAND.
I TUCKED THE BLADE INTO MY WAIST
WHEN I FIRST HEARD DEATH'S VOICE.
"YOU AND THE BLADE ARE NOW AS ONE
IN THAT YOU HAVE NO CHOICE."

TRACEY ROBINSON

I SHOOK DEATH'S HAND,

WHICH WASN'T COLD

AS I THOUGHT IT WOULD BE,

BUT THERE WAS NO DEPTH TO DEATH'S EYES,

AT LEAST NONE I COULD SEE.

"I CALLED FOR YOU TONIGHT

MY FRIEND,

I SENSED YOU'VE BEEN DISTRAUGHT."

I NEVER KNEW DEATH HAD THE GIFT

OF SENSING HUMAN THOUGHT.

I STORED AWAY THAT TIDBIT

TO BE USED JUST IN CASE

I FACED ANOTHER DEATHLING

IN SOME UNGODLY PLACE.

"YOU MUST BE VERY BUSY,"

I TOLD DEATH WITH A SIGH.

"I JUST CAN'T UNDERSTAND THE REASON

THAT SO MANY HAD TO DIE."

"THAT ANSWER IS BEYOND ME,"

DEATH TOLD ME IN RETURN

"AT TIMES LIKE THIS

THE DEATHLINGS RISE

TO FEED

TO KILL

TO BURN.

IT'S HAPPENED ON THE EARTH BEFORE

WHEN MANY HUMANS DIED.
I CAN'T CONTROL ALL DEATHLINGS,
ALTHOUGH AT TIMES I'VE TRIED."
IT WAS THEN I HEARD A MOANING,
I SAW A FLASHING TAIL,
AND UP FROM THE DEEP WATERS ROSE
A BEAUTIFUL BLUE WHALE.
DEATH HAD BROUGHT ME HERE BEFORE,
BENEATH THIS STARRY SKY,
FOR HERE IS WHERE THE BLUE WHALES COME
WHEN IT WAS TIME TO DIE.
"THE LEGEND OF THE SPIRIT BLADE
SAYS THAT IF YOU CONQUER DEATH
YOU EARN ANOTHER HUNDRED YEARS
BEFORE YOUR LAST
LIFE'S BREATH."
I THOUGHT ABOUT WHAT DEATH JUST SAID
AND WHAT THAT MEANT TO ME.
I CLOSED MY EYES,
AND BOWED MY HEAD,
AND THOUGHT OF WHAT COULD BE.
A HUNDRED EXTRA YEARS ON EARTH!
I LOOKED UP AT THE SKY.
HOW MANY FRIENDS WOULD PASS AWAY?
AND WOULD I WATCH THEM DIE?
IS THIS THE CURSE THAT DEATH ENDURES,

TRACEY ROBINSON

THE PASSING OF ALL SOULS?
HOW MANY TIMES WILL WE MEET HERE
TO WATCH THE WHALE'S LAST DANCE?
HOW MANY TIMES WILL I SENSE DEATH
AND KNOW IT IN ADVANCE?
I TOOK ONE LONG
LAST LOOK AROUND
AS BLUE WHALES ROSE TO SING.
I WONDERED MORE OF LIFE AND DEATH,
AND WHAT EACH ONE SHALL BRING.
WE SAT THERE
IN THAT MAGIC PLACE
HIGH ATOP THE WORLD,
THE PLACE WHERE BLUE WHALES GO TO DIE
AND TRUTH MAY BE UNFURLED.

THE 'PLUS' SIDE OF LIFE

FOR EVERY LIFE THAT'S LOST TODAY
ANOTHER CHILD IS BORN.
FOR EVERY LOVE AFFAIR THAT BLOOMS
ANOTHER HEART IS TORN.
FOR EVERY MAN WHO'S GIVEN UP
AND STARTS TO GO ASTRAY,
ANOTHER MAN LOOKS DEEP WITHIN
AND STARTS TO FIND HIS WAY.
FOR EVERY ANGEL DONNING WINGS
AND SLOWLY TAKING FLIGHT,
A MONSTER RISES QUIETLY
AND WALKS INTO THE NIGHT.
EVERY TIME I MAKE AMENDS
FOR UNFORGOTTEN SINS,
I TAKE ANOTHER STEP AWAY
FROM WHAT I COULD HAVE BEEN.

TRACEY ROBINSON

THE PRICE I PAY

I THANK THE PASSING SPIRITS
FOR WHISPERING TO ME,
FOR POEMS THAT THEY'VE HELPED ME WRITE,
AND ALL I'VE COME TO SEE.
I LIVE IN TRANSFORMATION,
I CHANGE AS DAYS GO BY.
IT SEEMS I HAVE BEEN BORN AGAIN,
I KNOW NOT HOW OR WHY.
FOR ALL THE BLESSINGS I'VE RECEIVED,
FOR ALL THAT I'VE BEEN SHOWN,
IT SEEMS THE PRICE THAT I MUST PAY
IS TO BE LEFT ALONE.
TO NEVER KNOW A WOMAN'S KISS,
TO NEVER HOLD HER TIGHT,
TO WAKE UP FROM A FITFUL DREAM
ON ANY GIVEN NIGHT.
THE DEATH OF ALL RELATIONSHIPS,
THE PASSING OF A FRIEND,
ALL THE TIMES I'VE FALLEN DOWN
AND RISEN UP AGAIN.
AND SO I SIT IN MOURNING

FOR PART OF ME HAS DIED.
THE PRICE I PAY
FOR GIFT'S RECEIVED
AND ALL THE TIMES I'VE TRIED.

THE PUPPETEER

I FEEL JUST LIKE A PUPPET,
A SMALL MARIONETTE.
I'VE SEEN SOME THINGS IN MY LIFETIME
I WISH I COULD FORGET.
THE STRINGS THAT MOVE MY ARMS AND LEGS
HAVE BEEN PULLED BY THE BEST
RECIDIVISM, SELF-HATRED—
YOU CAN ASSUME THE REST.
SOME PEOPLE'S STRINGS ARE TUGGED UPON
BY HABITS THEY'VE ACQUIRED,
WHILE OTHERS DANCE UPON LIFE'S STAGE
IN SEARCH OF WHAT'S DESIRED.
I'VE ALSO FELT WHAT IT IS LIKE
WHEN FORTUNE PULLS THE STRINGS.
YOU'VE ALL BEEN SAVED FROM DANGER AND
MORE UNFORTUNATE THINGS.
WHEN BULLETS FLEW RIGHT AT ME
IN THAT SMALL, CONFINED SPACE,
I FELT MY STRINGS PULLED TO AND FRO,
I WAS SAVED FROM DEATH'S EMBRACE.
I'VE CUT THE STRINGS OF IGNORANCE,

ALLOWING ME TO SEE
THE THOUGHTS I HELD SO LONG AGO
AND THEIR EFFECTS ON ME.
THE STRINGS OF LIFE CONNECT ME NOW,
I DANCE UPON LIFE'S STAGE.
MY HEART'S NOW FILLED WITH EMPATHY
WHERE ONCE IT BEAT WITH RAGE.
YOU MAY FEEL INDEPENDENT
BUT LET ME MAKE THIS CLEAR,
OUR DESTINIES LIE IN THE HANDS
OF A MASTER PUPPETEER.

TRACEY ROBINSON

THE SLEEPING SOLDIER

I SAW A SLEEPING SOLDER
AS I TRAVELED ON A TRAIN.
I WANTED TO AWAKEN HIM
THOUGH I TRIED HARD TO REFRAIN.
I THOUGHT OF HIS DEPLOYMENT,
WHERE IN THE WORLD HE'D GO.
ARE SOLDIERS TOLD AHEAD OF TIME
OR ARE THEY THE LAST TO KNOW?
THE WORLD IS IN SUCH TURMOIL
WITH TERROR IN THE AIR,
OUR SOLDIERS BEING SENT TO WAR,
NO COMPROMISES THERE.
I THOUGHT OF THAT YOUNG SOLDIER.
WHAT OF HIS FAMILY?
WAS WHATEVER THEY SAW IN HIM
THE LAST THAT THEY WOULD SEE?
WOULD HE FIGHT ON COURAGEOUSLY?
WOULD HE LOSE ANY FRIENDS?
WOULD HE BE THE TYPE OF SOLDIER ON WHOM
OTHERS RELY AND DEPEND?
WOULD HE DIE AS A HERO?

WOULD HE SURVIVE THE WAR?
AND THROUGH IT ALL
WOULD HE BE TOLD
JUST WHAT HE WAS FIGHTING FOR?
WHEN I REACHED MY DESTINATION
BEFORE I WALKED AWAY,
I SAID A PRAYER
AND HOPED THAT HE
WOULD RETURN SAFE ONE DAY.

TRACEY ROBINSON

THE SOULS THAT SURROUND ME

I MENTIONED TO YOU EARLIER
THAT THINGS WOULD SOON GET DEEP,
AND NOW I SIT
WITH PEN IN HAND
STILL UNABLE TO SLEEP.
I THOUGHT I SAW A SHADOW
FLICKER ACROSS THE ROOM.
IT DANCED FOR JUST A MOMENT,
THEN RETREATED TO THE GLOOM.
I FEEL THE SPIRITS' PRESENCE,
THOUGH THEY HAVE YET TO SPEAK.
I WONDER IF I'LL HAVE TO ASK
FOR ANSWERS THAT I SEEK.
I LISTEN VERY CAREFULLY
IN HOPES THAT I WILL HEAR
THE VOICE OF SOMEONE WHOM I'D LOST
WHISPERING INTO MY EAR.
IF EVERYONE COULD VISIT
BOTH FRIEND AND FAMILY,
A ROOM OF LOVING SPIRITS,
THEIR SOULS SURROUNDING ME.

THE WATCHER

I AM KNOWN AS THE WATCHER,
THOUGH THAT IS NOT MY NAME.
THERE IS NO RECORD OF MY BIRTH
OR FROM WHICH WORLD I CAME.
UPON AN ASTRAL MOUNTAINTOP
WITH ALL PLANETS IN VIEW,
I WATCH EVENTS FROM ALL THE WORLDS,
I SEE ALL THAT YOU DO.
I AM HOWEVER HELPLESS
TO ACT IN ANY WAY,
FOR I AM BOUND BY HOLY LAW
IN WHAT I DO AND SAY.
I SEE YOU AT THE BEST OF TIMES
WHEN HUMANITY PREVAILS.
I'VE ALSO SEEN YOUR MONSTERS AND
WHEN HUMAN JUSTICE FAILS.
I DO NOT SIT IN JUDGEMENT
AND I CAN PLACE NO BLAME.
ALTHOUGH YOU ALL ARE DIFFERENT,
I WATCH YOU JUST THE SAME.
I SEE THE LIFE ON EVERY WORLD,

TRACEY ROBINSON

AND IT IS STRANGE TO SEE
SO MANY BEINGS FAR AWAY,
HOW ALIKE THEY SEEM TO BE.
THE UNIVERSE IS FULL OF WAR
FOR EVERY PLANET FIGHTS.
SOME FOR WHAT THEY KNOW IS WRONG
AND OTHERS FOR WHAT'S RIGHT.
AT TIMES I FEEL GREAT SADNESS
AT WHAT I HAVE TO SEE,
THE RISE AND FALL OF PLANETS THAT
ALL ROTATE BEFORE ME.
I HAVE BEEN IN POSITION
SINCE BEFORE TIME BEGAN.
I'VE WITNESSED ALL THE HISTORY,
THE RISE AND FALL OF MAN
FROM GARDENS KNOWN AS EDEN
TO PROJECT TENEMENTS,
TO ALL THE THINGS THAT MAN HOLDS DEAR
AND WHAT THAT REPRESENTS.
I'VE SEEN YOUR ROCKETS TRY TO REACH
A DISTANCE YOU CAN'T GO.
I HAVE FORGOTTEN MANY THINGS
THAT MAN WILL NEVER KNOW.
I AM KNOWN AS THE WATCHER
AND I WATCH OVER YOU.
I SEE THE WAY YOU LIVE YOUR LIVES,
I SEE ALL THAT YOU DO.

THE 'YIN AND YANG' OF LIFE

A UNIVERSE OF PLANETS
EACH WITH ITS GRAVITY,
A PASSING THOUGHT IS NOTHING MORE
THAN SOME EPIPHANY.
FOR EVERY TIME THAT WE SUCCEED
THERE COMES ANOTHER LOSS.
LIFE'S BALANCED BY THE PRICES PAID
AND VARIANCE OF COST.
FOR EVERY SINGLE LIFE THAT ENDS
ANOTHER CHILD IS BORN,
FOR EVERY COUPLE SHARING LOVE
ANOTHER HEART IS TORN.
WE ALL LIVE IN GOD'S PLAYPEN
AS TOYS TO ENTERTAIN.
IF WE COULD CONCEIVE OF THE TRUTH
WE ALL WOULD GO INSANE.
FOR EVERY TRUE RELATIONSHIP
ANOTHER IS BETRAYED,
FOR EVERY MILESTONE MAN HAS REACHED
ANOTHER IS DELAYED.
FOR EVERY ACT OF GOODNESS

TRACEY ROBINSON

PERFORMED BY ANYONE,
A SIN'S ALSO COMMITTED AND
THAT DEED CAN'T BE UNDONE.
FOR EACH MAN LOST IN DARKNESS
ANOTHER SEES THE LIGHT.
FOR EACH PERSON THAT DOESN'T CARE,
ANOTHER DOES WHAT'S RIGHT.
THE YIN AND YANG OF LIFE WE KNOW,
THE PROMISES WE KEEP.
THE SEEDS OF LIFE WHICH WE ALL SOW,
WE LIVE WITH WHAT WE REAP.

THIS PAIN

IN THE TIME THAT IT HAS TAKEN ME
TO WRITE THESE WORDS TO YOU
A CHILD HAS DIED,
AND WE DON'T KNOW
THE PAIN IT WAS PUT THROUGH.
I FEEL IT
LIKE AN INNER ACHE,
A PAIN THAT SEEMS TO RISE.
I FEEL TIGHTNESS IN MY CHEST
AS TEARS SWELL IN MY EYES.
IS THE CUP HALF EMPTY,
OR IS IT HALFWAY FULL?
WITH HALF A CHANCE TO SAVE A CHILD
WOULD I BE CAPABLE?
I BEAR THE WEIGHT OF TROUBLED SOULS,
THEIR STORIES PLAGUE MY MIND.
I LONG TO EXORCISE MYSELF
AND LEAVE THIS PAIN BEHIND.

TRACEY ROBINSON

THIS 'RIDE OF LIFE'

OKAY KIDS,
STAY BUCKLED IN.
THERE'S MUCH MORE TO THIS RUN!
WITH UPS AND DOWNS AND WINDING CURVES
OUR RIDE HAS JUST BEGUN!
LIKE SOME WILD ROLLERCOASTER.
WE'VE RIDDEN UP AND DOWN
SINCE I HEARD VOICES IN MY HEAD
WHILE NO ONE WAS AROUND.
ON STRAIGHTAWAYS
WE COUNTED DAYS
AND WATCHED THE SCENERY,
WHILE WORDS ABOUND
AS TRUTH'S UNFOUND
AND SPIRITS SPOKE TO ME.
WE ALMOST THREW UP WHEN WE FELT
A SUDDEN JERKY RIDE.
OUR CARS TOOK A DIP UP AND DOWN
AND BANGED FROM SIDE TO SIDE.
THAT WAS WHEN WE RODE PAST DEATH,
THE DARKEST LENGTH OF TRACK.

HE STOLE OUR FRIENDS AND RELATIVES
AND WE CAN'T GET THEM BACK.
WE RODE ALONG IN SILENCE THEN,
WHICH LASTED FOR A BIT,
THEN EACH ONE FELT THEIR OWN CAR RISE,
EACH SPIRIT ROSE WITH IT.
WE OVERCAME OUR OBSTACLES,
WE REACHED OUR HIGHEST PEAK.
WE REACHED OUT FOR THE SUN
AS ONE
AND LET OUR SPIRITS SPEAK.
AND AS WE TOOK THE STEEP RIDE DOWN
WE SCREAMED,
WE LAUGHED,
WE CRIED.
WE RELISHED THIS,
THIS RIDE OF LIFE,
FOR ALL THE REASONS WHY.
AND WHEN WE REACHED ITS BOTTOM
WE STILL RODE STRAIGHT AND TRUE.
FOR ON LIFE'S RIDE
THERE ARE NO STOPS
UNTIL YOUR RIDE IS THROUGH.
SOME OF US MAY HAVE TO GET OFF
WHEN WE PASS DEATH AGAIN.
FOR THOSE OF YOU

TRACEY ROBINSON

WHO DON'T PASS THROUGH,
"RIDE ON IN PEACE
MY FRIEND."
TO THOSE OF YOU WITH LENGTHY RIDES,
BEFORE YOUR TIME IS DONE,
BE YOUR BEST,
DO YOUR BEST,
AND LEAVE NO DEED UNDONE.

TO EVERYONE I SAY A PRAYER

TO EVERYONE WHO JUST WOKE UP
AND FELT THEY WERE ALONE,
TO EVERYONE WHO JUST FOUND OUT,
THEY'D LOST A FRIEND THEY'D KNOWN.
TO EVERYONE WHO IS AFRAID
GOD MAY HAVE TURNED HIS BACK,
TO EVERYONE WHO STRUGGLES HARD
AND TRIES TO STAY ON TRACK.
TO EVERYONE WHO WATCHED THE NEWS
AND TURNED OFF THE TV,
DEPRESSED TO THINK THAT MANKIND HAS
LOST ALL HUMANITY.
TO EVERYONE WHO WALKS ALONE
UPON THE ROAD OF LIFE,
TO EVERY HUSBAND WAKING UP
SO GRATEFUL FOR A WIFE.
TO EVERYONE WHO STILL BELIEVES
IN POSSIBILITY.
TO EVERY OPEN PRISON DOOR
THAT SETS A CHANGED MAN FREE.

TRACEY ROBINSON

TO EVERYONE THAT STOPS TO WATCH
THE RISING OF THE SUN.
TO EVERY CHASER OF A DREAM,
A NEW DAY HAS BEGUN.
TO EVERYONE WHO STARES UP AT
THE STARS WHICH LIGHT THE SKY.
TO EVERYONE WHO FEELS GREAT PAIN
BUT THEN REFUSES TO CRY.
TO EVERYONE I SAY A PRAYER,
I HOPE WILL HELP YOU FIND,
IF NOT THE ANSWERS THAT YOU SEEK,
AT LEAST SOME PEACE OF MIND.
I PRAY THE SUN SHINES DOWN ON YOU
AND WARMS YOU WITH ITS RAYS,
AND THAT REGARDLESS OF YOUR PAST
YOU LIVE THROUGH BETTER DAYS.
I PRAY YOU ARE REMEMBERED
FOR ALL THE GOOD YOU'VE DONE,
THAT SPECIAL MEMORIES OF YOU
ARE SHARED BY EVERYONE.
I PRAY YOU SEE A RAINBOW
THAT LEAPS ACROSS THE SKY
AND THAT YOU KNOW IT'S MEANT FOR YOU
AND ALL THE REASONS WHY.
I PRAY FOR ALL YOUR FAMILIES
AND BONDS THAT YOU STILL SHARE.

I PRAY EACH DAY YOUR CHILDREN KNOW
YOU LOVE THEM AND YOU CARE.
I PRAY YOU HEAR THE SPIRITS
THAT WHISPER QUIETLY.
THEY SPEAK OF THINGS YOU'VE YET TO KNOW
AND THINGS YOU'VE YET TO SEE.

TRACEY ROBINSON

TRUE DEFINITION

FOR EVERYONE WHO SITS AT HOME
AFTER A LONG, HARD DAY,
WHOSE CHILDREN MAY BE SLEEPING
IN ROOMS NOT FAR AWAY;
FOR EVERYONE WHO'S LOST IN THOUGHT
ON HOW THEIR ENDS THEY'LL MEET,
WHO MAY HAVE TAKEN SEVERAL BLOWS
BUT NEVER KNOWN DEFEAT;
FOR EVERYONE WHO'S CHANGED A LIFE
WITH GESTURE OR WITH WORD;
FOR EVERYONE WHO'S PASSED ALONG
SOME WISDOM THAT THEY'VE HEARD;
FOR EVERYONE WITH COURAGE
WHO STANDS UP FOR THE WEAK;
FOR EVERYONE WHO VENTURES FORTH
FOR ANSWERS THAT THEY SEEK;
FOR EVERYONE WHO'S NOT AFRAID
TO SOMETIMES SIT AND WEEP;
FOR EVERYONE WHO'S KNOWN FOR ALL
THE PROMISES THEY KEEP;
FOR EVERYONE WHO BALANCES

RESPONSIBILITIES;
FOR EVERYONE WHO HURTS BUT WILL
NOT LET THEIR CHILDREN SEE:
YOU ARE THE GREATEST BEINGS,
THE HIGHEST FORM OF LIFE.
YOU MIGHT BE SINGLE AND NOT HAVE
A HUSBAND OR A WIFE,
BUT YOU ARE THE BAROMETER
BY WHICH ALL OF MANKIND
IS MEASURED, AND INDEED HOW WE
ARE TRUTHFULLY DEFINED.

TRACEY ROBINSON

WHAT DOES IT MEAN

WHAT DOES IT MEAN
FOR ONE TO BE
A CHILD OF GOD TODAY?
ALTHOUGH QUITE HARD TO QUANTIFY
I SIT, AND THINK, AND PRAY.
I PRAY IT MEANS THAT ONE FEELS JOY
AT ALL LIFE'S MAJESTY;
I PRAY THAT PEOPLE STRIVE TO RISE
TO ALL THAT THEY CAN BE.
I PRAY THAT GOD IS SEEN AS MORE
THAN ANY BOOK MAY TELL,
THAT THOSE NOT MEMBERS OF A CHURCH
MAY SPEAK TO HIM AS WELL.
I PRAY THAT PEOPLE REALIZE
THAT ALL OF LIFE HAS FORCE,
AN ENERGY CONTROLLING THINGS,
ALL LIFE, AND US OF COURSE.
WITHOUT DENOMINATION
CAN ANYONE STILL PRAY?
AND HOW COULD ANY OF US KNOW
GOD HEARS THE WORDS WE SAY?

AND WHAT ABOUT THE PEOPLE
WHO SAY THEY DON'T BELIEVE?
HOW IS IT THAT THEY RECONCILE
THE BLESSINGS THEY RECEIVE?
WE ALL WITNESS DISASTER
EACH OF US DEALS WITH PAIN;
WE'VE ALSO SEEN THE RAINBOWS RISE
AFTER THE STRONGEST RAIN.
TO ME, TO BE A CHILD OF GOD
MEANS I'M FINALLY ABLE TO SEE
THAT AFTER ALL THAT I'VE BEEN THROUGH,
THE SUN STILL SHINES ON ME.

TRACEY ROBINSON

WHAT IF?

WHAT IF THE WORLD WE LIVED IN
WERE ONE WITHOUT GOODBYES?
WHERE LOVED ONES NEVER PASSED AWAY
WATCHED THROUGH OUR TEARFUL EYES?
WHAT IF THE FORCE OF KARMA
AND THE LAWS OF CIRCUMSTANCE
ALL TENDED TOWARDS ENDS THAT
GAVE HUMANITY HALF A CHANCE?
WHAT IF EVERYONE ELSE COULD HEAR
THE WORDS I HEAR RIGHT NOW?
COULD SPIRITS' WHISPERS CHANGE THE WORLD,
AND IF THEY COULD, THEN HOW?
WHAT IF ALL PEOPLE TOLD THE TRUTH
AND NO ONE EVER LIED?
WHAT IF WE ALL ACHIEVED SUCCESS
FOR EACH TIME THAT WE TRIED?
WHAT IF EVERY RELATIONSHIP
WAS STRONG AND LOYAL AND TRUE,
WHERE NO CHILDREN ARE LEFT BEHIND
WHEN LOVE AFFAIRS ARE THROUGH?
I OFTEN WONDER OF THESE THINGS,

AS WELL AS MANY MORE,
JUST AS I WONDER WHAT IT IS
THAT I WAS GIFTED FOR.

TRACEY ROBINSON

WHAT THOSE WHISPERS MEANT

I HATE WHEN THIS THING HAPPENS,
BUT IT HAPPENS ALL THE TIME:
THE PAIN THAT SOMEONE ELSE MUST FEEL
IS SUDDENLY NOW MINE.
IT DOESN'T FEEL LIKE VIOLENCE,
IT DOESN'T FEEL LIKE DEATH.
MY CHEST DOES NOT FEEL CRUSHED
AS IF I'D TAKEN MY LAST BREATH.
IT DOESN'T FEEL LIKE CHILD ABUSE,
I DO NOT HEAR THAT SCREAM,
ALTHOUGH MY EYES NOW RUN WITH TEARS,
AND I DON'T KNOW WHAT THAT MEANS.
HAS SOMEONE'S HEART BEEN BROKEN?
WAS SOMEONE MADE A FOOL?
DID SOME FAST CAR
HIT SOME YOUNG KID
WALKING HOME FROM SCHOOL?
THESE INSTANCES
THEY COME AND GO,
I DON'T KNOW HOW OR WHEN,

UNTIL THE TIMES I LOSE CONTROL
AND IT HAPPENS AGAIN.
I AM A MAN WHO IS POSSESSED
WHEN SPIRITS COME TO CALL.
THEY'VE LIFTED ME TO GREATER HEIGHTS
AND NEVER LET ME FALL.
I ALWAYS PRAY FOR WHO IT IS
WHO BEARS THAT BRUNT OF PAIN,
THOUGH I DO NOT KNOW WHERE THEY ARE
NOR DO I KNOW THEIR NAMES.
I WALK THE STREETS AT NIGHT, AT TIMES
I STARE INTO THE DARK.
I CHECK THE ALLEY'S SHADOWS AND
I CHECK THE EMPTY PARK.
I SEARCH TO SAVE A VICTIM,
I SEARCH FOR MONSTERS TOO.
IF I COME ACROSS ONE HUNTING THEN
YOU ALL KNOW WHAT I'LL DO.
I CARRY MANY WEAPONS,
ALL OF WHICH REPRESENT
THE SPIRITS' WHISPERS THAT I HEAR,
AND WHAT THOSE WHISPERS MEANT.

TRACEY ROBINSON

WHEN IT'S TIME

WHEN SOMEONE IS ABOUT TO DIE
DO THEY SOMETIMES JUST KNOW?
IS THERE A SIGN THAT THEY RECEIVE
THAT SAYS IT'S TIME TO GO?
OR DO WE SOMETIMES JUST SHUT DOWN
LIKE A TURNED OFF MACHINE?
AND ARE OUR MEMORIES
THE VERY LAST THING THAT WE'VE SEEN?
AND WHAT OF ALL OUR SECRETS,
THE THINGS THAT JUST WE KNOW,
THE HABITS THAT WE OFTEN HIDE,
OR PLACES THAT WE GO?
WILL SOMEONE FIND THOSE CIGARETTES
YOU PROMISED NOT TO SMOKE?
WILL YOUR LOVED ONES BE QUITE UPSET
OR THINK IT A CRUEL JOKE?
WHAT OF THAT LIQUOR BOTTLE
YOU HID UNDER THE BED?
WILL THEY BE MAD TO SEE YOU DRANK
IN SPITE OF WHAT YOU SAID?
WILL SOMEONE FIND YOUR DIARY

AND SIT TO READ YOUR THOUGHTS?
WILL THEY COME ACROSS OLD RECEIPTS
OF EVERYTHING YOU'VE BOUGHT?
WHEN IT IS TIME TO PASS AWAY
DO SPIRITS GATHER ROUND
TO WELCOME YET ANOTHER SOUL
A NEW FRIEND THAT THEY'VE FOUND?
WILL WE LAY FEELING PARALYZED
AND UNABLE TO MOVE,
OR WILL WE JUST RELAX AND GO
WITH NOTHING LEFT TO PROVE?
I SIT HERE AND I CONTEMPLATE
THE WAYS OF LIFE AND DEATH,
JUST WONDERING HOW I WILL FEEL
WHEN I TAKE MY LAST BREATH.
ONE THING THAT I AM CERTAIN OF
IS WHEN MY LIFE IS THROUGH
THE LAST THOUGHTS RUNNING THROUGH MY HEAD
WILL BE OF ALL OF YOU.

TRACEY ROBINSON

WHEN THE SPIRITS SPEAK TO ME

MY HEART IS STILL AFLUTTER,
MY SOUL BEGINS TO RISE.
I'M DANCING TO A RHYTHM
OF THE WORDS BEHIND MY EYES.
A SHOOTING STAR'S WITHIN ME,
IT SHOOTS ACROSS MY CHEST:
THE THINGS THE SPRITS LET ME SEE
WHEN I BECOME POSSESSED.
I NO LONGER FEEL LONELINESS,
I'M LOST WITHIN THEIR WORLD.
I SEE THE WORLD FOR WHAT IT IS,
I SEE THE TRUTH UNFURLED.
ALAS, THE FEELING ISN'T LONG;
I'M STARTING TO BELIEVE
THAT SPIRITS HAVE A CERTAIN TIME
WHEN THEY ALL HAVE TO LEAVE.
ALTHOUGH I ALWAYS WRITE TO YOU
OF PLEASANT, THOUGHTFUL VERSE,
I ALSO HEAR WHEN EVIL SPEAKS
AND THEREIN LIES MY CURSE.

I WRITE TO YOU OF MONSTERS
AND SOME OF WHAT THEY DO,
BUT THAT'S BECAUSE I LISTEN AND
WRITE WHAT THEY SAY TO YOU.
EVIL IS A LIFE FORCE
AND THOUGH IT RIDES ON AIR,
IT CARRIES WITH IT MANY SCENTS,
SOME OF WHICH ARE HARD TO BEAR.
I TRY NOT TO ALARM YOU,
FOR YOU DO NOT NEED TO SEE
THE MANY HORRORS I ENDURE
WHEN SPIRITS SPEAK TO ME.

TRACEY ROBINSON

WHEN YOU LOOK AT ME AGAIN

THEY SAY YOU SOMETIMES CANNOT SEE
THE FOREST FOR THE TREES.
THIS HAPPENS QUITE ROUTINELY WHEN
SOMEBODY LOOKS AT ME.
THE TREES THAT BLOCK YOUR VISION
ARE REMNANTS OF MY PAST.
THEY BLOCK YOUR VIEW FOR JUST AS LONG
AS THOSE MEMORIES LAST.
YOU COULD NOT SEE THE MAN BELOW
OR WHAT I FELT INSIDE.
YOU ONLY SAW THE TIMES I'VE FAILED,
NOT ALL THE TIMES I'VE TRIED.
THE TREETOPS BLOCKED MY SIGHT AS WELL.
I COULD NOT SEE THE SKY,
WHILE MONSTERS STALKED DURING THE NIGHT
AND I NEVER KNEW WHY.
BELOW THE FOREST'S CANOPY
I LIVED, I LAUGHED, I LOVED,
NEVER SEEING RAINBOWS WHICH
TRAVERSED BRIGHT SKIES ABOVE.

WHEN YOU LOOK AT ME AGAIN
LOOK DEEPER, PAST THE TREES,
FOR THERE, UPON THE FOREST FLOOR,
ALONE, IS WHERE I'LL BE.

TRACEY ROBINSON

WILL I EVER BE THE SAME?

DO SUMMER FLOWERS SOMETIMES CRY
WHEN THE SEASONS CHANGE TO FALL?
WHO DO THE MOUNTAINS CRY OUT TO,
WHEN THEY FEEL THAT THEY MIGHT FALL?
DO RIVERS CURRENTS CHANGE THEIR COURSE,
DO SEAS ALTER THEIR TIDES?
AND WHERE DOES DANGER TURN TO
IF MORE DANGER SHOULD ARISE?
WHERE DOES PEACE RETREAT TO
WHEN MAN RESORTS TO WAR?
AND WHEN IT'S DONE
DO WE STILL KNOW
WHAT WE WERE FIGHTING FOR?
THREE DAYS OF VENTILATION
I'D FORGOTTEN MY NAME.
I SIT. I CRY. I WONDER IF
I'LL EVER BE THE SAME.

A BREAKFAST WITH DEATH

I ATE BREAKFAST WITH DEATH TODAY.
WE MET UP AT SUNRISE.
I SAW THAT HE'D BEEN BUSY
—FATIGUE WAS IN HIS EYES.
I ASKED HIM HOW HE FELT ABOUT
HOW MANY LIVES WERE LOST,
THE STATE OF EARTH'S PANDEMIC
AND IT'S HIGH, UNGODLY COST.
DEATH TOOK A QUIET MOMENT
BEFORE HE CHOSE TO SPEAK:
"I'M NOT SURE THAT I CAN PROVIDE
THE ANSWERS THAT YOU SEEK."
DEATH TOOK A SIP OF COFFEE,
AND THEN A BITE OF FOOD.
I HOPED THE QUESTION THAT I ASKED
HAD NOT UPSET HIS MOOD.
"I STARTED OUT AS YOU DID,"
DEATH SAID IN A LOW TONE.
"LIKE YOU, I SPENT MOST OF MY DAYS
IN THOUGHTAND ALL ALONE."
I LOOKED AT DEATH

AND ASKED MYSELF,
"JUST HOW OLD MUST DEATH BE?"
DEATH SAID,
"SEVERAL HUNDRED THOUSAND YEARS,"
AS HE SMILED DOWN AT ME.
"I TOO HEARD THE SPIRITS
BUT MY GIFT WAS NOT OF VERSE.
I CAN'T CALL IT A 'GIFT' AT ALL,
FOR IT SEEMS MORE A CURSE."
I THOUGHT ON THAT:
SO MANY SOULS,
OVER THOUSANDS OF YEARS;
SO MANY BROKEN FAMILIES;
SO MANY HEARTFELT TEARS.
"AND SO IT WAS ASSIGNED TO ME,
THE SOLEMN TASK I DO.
I'VE NEVER FOUND A FRIEND IN MAN
UNTIL IT CAME TO YOU.
WE'VE SEEN EACH OTHER MANY TIMES
EACH TIME, TO MY SURPRISE,
I SAW YOU RISE UP GALANTLY,
AND EACH TIME YOU SURVIVED."
I HADN'T SEEN DEATH AT THOSE TIMES
BUT HE WAS THERE, I KNOW.
SOME OF THOSE TIMES I HAD FELT FEAR
WHICH I DID NOT LET SHOW.

"NOT EVERYBODY FEARS ME,"
DEATH SAID, AND ATE SOME MORE.
"YOU'D BE SURPRISED AT ALL THE ONES
WHO'VE KNOCKED UPON DEATH'S DOOR.
SOME PEOPLE LIVE A LONG, GOOD LIFE,
AND WHEN THAT LIFE MUST END,
WHETHER OR NOT THEY WELCOME ME
MAY REALLY JUST DEPEND.
DEPENDS ON THEIR LIFE'S CHOICES,
THE FRIENDS THEY WORKED TO MAKE,
THE GOALS THAT THEY SET FOR THEMSELVES,
CHANCES THEY CHOSE TO TAKE."
"BUT WHAT ABOUT THE CHILDREN?"
I ASKED DEATH SUDDENLY.
"WHAT OF THE MANY SOULS THAT SEEM
TO LEAVE MUCH TOO EARLY?"
DEATH LEANED BACK IN HIS CHAIR
AND SAID, "YES MY FRIEND, I MUST AGREE.
THOSE ARE THE WORST OF ALL:
SOME SOULS DON'T GET A CHANCE TO RISE
BEFORE THEY TAKE A FALL.
I'VE BEEN AROUND FOR MANY YEARS,"
MY FRIEND DEATH SAID TO ME,
"AND I HAVE YET TO UNDERSTAND
"SOME OF THE THINGS I SEE."
WE SAT IN SILENCE FOR A BIT,

TRACEY ROBINSON

FOR WE WERE BOTH IN THOUGHT.
I PRAYED FOR SPIRITS' WHISPERS
AND THE LESSONS WHICH THEY TAUGHT.
I ATE BREAKFAST WITH DEATH TODAY,
A MEAL SHARED WITH A FRIEND.
I KNEW THAT WE'D SHARE MANY MEALS
WHEN MY LIFE CAME TO AN END.
DEATH TOOK ME TO THE PLACE ONCE
WHERE BLUE WHALES GO TO DIE;
TODAY I CHOSE A PLACE WHERE DEATH
COULD SEE THE RICH BLUE SKY.

A BRIEF ENCOUNTER
WITH DEATH

DEATH APPROACHED ME YESTERDAY

AS I WALKED DOWN THE STREET.

I FELT SOME APPREHENSION

SINCE WE HAD NO PLANS TO MEET.

"PLEASE DON'T WORRY

MY GOOD FRIEND,"

DEATH SAID SOFTLY TO ME.

"I THOUGHT I SAW YOU FROM AFAR

AND CAME CLOSER TO SEE."

I LOOKED AT DEATH

AND HE LOOKED GAUNT.

I WONDERED HOW HE'D BEEN.

I KNOW THAT HE WAS BUSY WITH

THE STATE THE WORLD WAS IN.

DEATH LEANED AGAINST A BUILDING,

THEN HE LET OUT A SIGH,

BEFORE HE STOPPED TO WATCH A CROWD

OF PEOPLE PASSING BY.

"IF PEOPLE KNEW HOW OFTEN

THEY PASSED ME BY EACH DAY,

TRACEY ROBINSON

I WONDER HOW THEIR THOUGHTS WOULD CHANGE?

I WONDER WHAT THEY'D SAY?"

WE SPOKE SOME OF THE WEATHER

AND NEWS BRIEFS OF THE DAY,

THEN DEATH STRAIGHTENED UP

AND SAID, "MY FRIEND, I MUST BE ON MY WAY."

I WATCHED DEATH WALK OFF,

GETTING LOST IN THE CROWD

WHILE I THOUGHT OF WHAT I WANTED MOST:

TO WAKE UP TOMORROW, AND STILL BE ALIVE,

OR RAISE GLASSES WITH DEATH FOR A TOAST.

A DAY OF GRACE

I WISH THAT I COULD JUST BE FREE,
AT LEAST A LITTLE WHILE,
AND IF THERE IS A PENALTY
I'LL GLADLY RECONCILE.
SOME TIME WITHOUT THE VOICES,
THE WHISPERS AND THE SCREAMS.
SOME TIME WITHOUT VERSES OF TRUTH
AND WHAT THAT TRUTH MAY MEAN.
I WISH I COULD JUST SLEEP AWHILE
A DAY IN WHICH TO REST.
HAVE I NOT SHOWN MY FEALTY?
HAVE I NOT PASSED EACH TEST?
I WISH I COULD JUST DREAM AWHILE
YET STAY WITHIN MY WORLD
INSTEAD OF ALL THE OTHER STARS
WITH ALL THEIR TRUTHS UNFURLED.
I WISH I COULD TAKE A TRIP BACK,
A SHORT JOURNEY THROUGH TIME,
SO I COULD TALK A LITTLE WHILE
WITH LONG-LOST FRIENDS OF MINE.
I WISH THAT I COULD BE ALLOWED

TRACEY ROBINSON

TO SPEND SOME TIME ALONE,
TO CONTEMPLATE MY OWN THOUGHTS
AND ALL THAT WHICH I'VE BEEN SHOWN.
I WISH THE WOMAN OF MY DREAMS
WOULD TURN SO I COULD SEE
THE VASTNESS OF THE GIFT THAT GOD
HAS PUT IN PLACE FOR ME.
I'VE ACTUALLY SEEN HER FACE,
BUT SHE IS NOT AWARE
OF THE DEPTH OF MY FEELINGS
OR HOW DEEPLY I CARE.
I WISH I COULD JUST SIT AWHILE
IN SILENCE AND IN PEACE,
A DAY OF GRACE WITHIN MY MIND
AS ALL THE VOICES CEASE.

A LOOK INTO A MIRROR

A LOOK INTO A MIRROR
REFLECTS WHAT PEOPLE SEE,
ALTHOUGH WE ALL POSSESS A SECRET
PERSONALITY.
A PERSON'S INNER SPIRIT,
THAT WHOM THEY TRULY ARE:
SOME ARE CHARGED WITH NEWFOUND HOPE
AND OTHERS BLEED FROM SCARS.
SOME REFLECTIONS SHOW GOOD TRUTH
OF WHAT LIES IN THE HEART,
WHILE SOME REVEAL A MONSTER'S REIGN
THAT'S JUST WAITING TO START.
SOMETIMES THE PERSON THAT WE SEE
IS SOMEONE WE DON'T KNOW.
WE MIGHT MEET UP WITH THEM SOMETIME,
THOUGH WE'VE GOT SOME WAY TO GO.
THEY SAY THE EYES ARE WINDOWS
THAT LOOK INTO THE SOUL,
AND TEARS ARE JUST THE WAVES OF LIFE
WHICH CRASH UPON THE SHOALS.
OUR SECRET SELF WALKS WITH US.

TRACEY ROBINSON

LOOK CLOSELY AND YOU'LL SEE
THAT WHICH LIES DEEPEST IN YOUR HEART
AND ALL THAT YOU CAN BE.

A MOMENT'S THOUGHT

TONIGHT I THOUGHT OF SHOOTING STARS,
OF WORLDS LIGHT YEARS AWAY.
I WONDERED WHAT BEINGS WERE THERE
AND HOW THEY'D SPENT THEIR DAY.
WOULD SOME FATHER HAVE WORKED ALL DAY?
SOME MOTHER WORKED AS WELL?
WOULD CHILDREN
FROM ANOTHER WORLD
COME HOME WITH TALES TO TELL?
WOULD OTHER WORLDS HAVE CITIES
AND SUBURBS FOR THE RICH?
AND WHICH CURRENCY WOULD BE USED
TO DETERMINE WHICH WERE WHICH?
I KNOW THAT OTHER PLANETS
WOULD SHARE SIMILAR TRAITS
LIKE GREED, ENVY AND JEALOUSY,
RACISM AND HATE.
AS LONG AS THERE ARE LIVING THINGS,
THEN POWER WILL BE SOUGHT:
SOME BEINGS SUBJUGATED AND
SOME BEINGS WILL BE BOUGHT.

TRACEY ROBINSON

I KNOW EACH WORLD HAS HEROES
AND THOSE WHO SEEK WHAT'S RIGHT,
STRONG BEINGS REPRESENTING TRUTH,
AND FOR IT THEY WOULD FIGHT.
THE YOUNGEST ON OTHER PLANETS
WOULD BE THEIR GREATEST JEWELS,
BUT CHILDREN ON ALL OTHER WORLDS
LEARN SOMETIMES LIFE IS CRUEL.
I THOUGHT OF OTHER WORLDS TONIGHT
AND WONDERED IF UP THERE,
THE SPIRITS OF THE BEINGS PAST
STILL WHISPERED IN THE AIR.

A MONSTER'S RIDE

ONCE AGAIN THEY TAKE ME
UPON A FRIGHTFUL RIDE.
SOMEHOW THEY MAKE THEIR THOUGHTS AND MINE
PRECISELY COINCIDE.
TONIGHT I FEEL THE HUNGER
OF SOME COLD
SAVAGE BEAST.
I FEEL ITS CRAVING FOR RAW FLESH,
I FEEL ITS NEED TO FEAST.
I TAKE A LOOK AROUND ME,
AND THOUGH THE ROOM IS BARE,
I AM WITHIN THE MONSTER,
AND WHERE IT IS, I'M THERE.
I CANNOT SEE THE BACKGROUND,
THERE'S NO ONE I CAN WARN
ALL I CAN DO IS SEE AND FEEL
AND SIT WITH FEELINGS TORN.
THIS IS ONE OF THOSE DARK NIGHTS
THAT I DON'T OFTEN SHARE.
I ONLY SPEAK OF SPIRITS,
NOT THE MONSTERS THAT ARE THERE.

TRACEY ROBINSON

BUT MONSTERS LIVE
AND WALK THE EARTH.
MOST LOOK LIKE YOU AND ME.
BUT A MONSTER'S LIVING SPIRIT,
THAT'S THE BEING THAT I SEE.
I SEE ITS VERY ESSENCE,
THE TRUTH IT TRIES TO HIDE.
TO YOU IT LOOKS QUITE HUMAN,
BUT THE MONSTER LIES INSIDE.
RIGHT NOW IT HAS BEEN WAITING,
IT CAN HARDLY HOLD IT BACK.
AT SOME POINT SOON IT WILL FIND PREY
AND THEN IT WILL ATTACK.
MONSTERS COME IN DIFFERENT BREEDS
LIKE DOGS AND CATS AND SUCH.
THE DIFFERENCES BETWEEN THEM
CAN VARY VERY MUCH.
SOME MONSTERS LIKE TO RAPE AND BEAT—
IT'S POWER THAT THEY SEEK—
WHILE OTHER MONSTERS JUST DESIRE
TO SUBJUGATE THE WEAK.
SOME MONSTERS PREY ON CHILDREN,
THEY ARE THE WORST OF ALL:
SOMEWHERE A CHILD WILL SUFFER WHEN
A MONSTER GETS THAT CALL.
SOME MONSTERS DO NOT COMMIT CRIMES,

THEY ACT IN LEGAL WAYS,
BUT THEY FEED ON THE THINGS THEY DO
TO DARKEN OTHER'S DAYS.
SOME MONSTERS HUNT ONLY TO KILL,
AND KILL IS WHAT THEY DO,
DISCARDING BODIES NEAR WATER
LIKE GARBAGE WHEN THEY'RE THROUGH.
THE MONSTER THAT I SEE RIGHT NOW
IS ONE WHO SEEKS TO KILL.
IT HASN'T BEEN SUSPECTED YET—
PERHAPS IT NEVER WILL.
I FEEL ITS NERVOUS TENSION,
I ALSO SMELL ITS FEAR.
I SEE THE THINGS THAT IT CAN SEE,
I HEAR WHAT IT CAN HEAR.
I WONDER IF THERE IS A WAY
THAT I MAY TRY TO SEE,
SOME SORT OF HINT OR CLUE OF WHERE
THIS MONSTER'S TAKEN ME.
I FEEL ITS MUSCLES TENSING,
IT CANNOT HOLD BACK LONG.
THE HUNGER IS A VOICE IT HEARS;
THE MONSTER LOVES ITS SONG.
I CANNOT SEE THE VICTIM
FROM HERE WITHIN ITS HEAD.
I FEAR THAT BY THE TIME I DO

TRACEY ROBINSON

IT ALREADY WILL BE DEAD.
I'VE SEEN SO MANY VICTIMS,
I'VE SEEN THE WAYS THEY DIE.
I'VE STOPPED AND TAKEN TIME TO LOOK
INTO THEIR LIFELESS EYES.
I'VE HEARD THE CHILDREN CRYING,
I'VE HEARD THE WOMEN'S SCREAMS,
AND WHEN I HEAR THE MONSTER'S SONG
I KNOW JUST WHAT IT MEANS.
I'VE HEARD THE MONSTER'S CRIES AS WELL.
IT CRIES IN GUILT AND PAIN.
IT FEELS REGRET THAT IT HAS KILLED
BUT IT SHALL KILL AGAIN.
SO THIS IS HOW I'LL SPEND TONIGHT,
IN THE DARK MIND OF A BEAST.
I HOPE THAT I AM SPARED THE SIGHT
OF HOW IT SOON WILL FEAST.

NEW YORK MINUTE

WHAT IS A "NEW YORK MINUTE"?
IT'S DANGER AT ITS WORST,
WHEN WHO SURVIVES MAY NOT DEPEND
ON WHO DREW THEIR GUN FIRST.
A LONELY GIRL ACCOSTED;
A MAN SOON TO BE ROBBED;
A MAN ABOUT TO MURDER BUT
TO HIM IT'S JUST A JOB.
IT MAY COME AS AN OVERT ACT
OR ONE OF CIRCUMSTANCE.
THE WAYS YOU MOVE DETERMINE
IF YOU EVEN HAVE A CHANCE.
THE FIRST KEY IS AWARENESS
OF ALL SURROUNDING YOU,
SO YOU WILL KNOW
WHICH WAY TO GO
AND WHAT THINGS YOU SHOULD DO.
WHENEVER YOU ENTER A MALL
NOTE PATHWAYS OF EGRESS,
ALL AVENUES OF ESCAPE
IN TIMES OF GREAT DISTRESS.

TRACEY ROBINSON

IS YOUR CAR WORKING PROPERLY?

DO YOUR TIRES HAVE GRIP?

WILL YOU RUN INTO DANGER

ON THE ROAD

WHILE ON YOUR TRIP?

WHO SURVIVES DISASTER?

WHO LIVES THROUGH ACCIDENTS?

WHO DECIDES

WHO LIVES OR DIES

AND HOW EACH CHOICE MAKES SENSE?

SO MANY PEOPLE DIE EACH DAY,

TOO MANY TO KEEP SCORE.

LIVE THROUGH YOUR

"NEW YORK MINUTE," SINCE

YOUR LIFE'S WORTH FIGHTING FOR.

ALL THE WORLDS A STAGE

IF I COULD STAND UPON A STAGE
AND SPEAK MY TRUTH TO YOU,
I WOULD NOT SPEAK OF ALL THE THINGS
THAT I'VE HAD TO LIVE THROUGH.
INSTEAD I'D TALK OF LESSONS,
THE THINGS THAT I HAVE LEARNED.
I'D SAY HOW HAPPY THAT I AM
FOR THE RESPECT I'VE EARNED.
I'D TALK OF MAN'S POTENTIAL,
HOW FAR WE COULD RISE,
AND I WOULD SPEAK OF QUALITIES
IN MAN THAT WE DESPISE.
THE WEIGHT THAT I HAVE CARRIED
WOULD DROP ME TO ONE KNEE,
BUT STILL I WOULD NOT CRY OUT FOR
HOW LIFE HAS TREATED ME.
WITH BRIGHT LIGHTS SHINING DOWN ON ME,
I'D STAND WITH MY BOWED HEAD.
I WOULD HOPE THAT MY AUDIENCE
REMEMBERS WHAT I SAID.
BEFORE I STOP AND TAKE A BOW

TRACEY ROBINSON

I'D SAY A SILENT PRAYER,
FOR ALL THE TRUTHS THAT I'VE BEEN TOLD
BY SPIRITS IN THE AIR.

BLESSINGS TO THE SPIRITS ABOUND

THANK YOU
TO THE SPIRITS
AND ALL THE THINGS THEY'VE SHOWN.
THANK YOU
FOR THE BLESSINGS
OF EACH SEED I HAVE SOWN.
THANK YOU
TO ALL OF MY FRIENDS
AND FOR THIS LIFE YOU'VE SAVED,
FOR EVERY ❤ THAT YOU'VE BESTOWED,
EACH OPINION YOU GAVE.
THANK YOU FOR THE AIR OF LIFE
SUSTAINING ME EACH DAY,
NOT TAINTING ME WITH A VIRUS THAT
TOOK MANY SOULS AWAY.
THANK YOU
TO THE MONSTERS
WHOM I HEAR,
I DON'T KNOW WHY:
I WILL FOREVER HUNT YOU

TRACEY ROBINSON

UNTIL I WATCH YOU DIE.
THANK YOU TO ALL OF THE SOULS
WHO VENTURE THROUGH THE GATE,
AND TRAVEL THE WORLD WITH BLESSINGS
THE ALTERING OF FATE.
THANK YOU
GOD
FOR SPARING ME
FROM ALL THE TIMES WHEN I FACED DEATH,
WHICH WASN'T MEANT TO BE.
THANKS FOR MY SURVIVAL,
AND THANK YOU FOR MY STRENGTH,
ALLOWING ME A SECOND CHANCE
TO LIVE LIFE TO ITS LENGTH.
I SIT WITH MY HEAD BENT IN PRAYER.
I WHISPER WHAT I SAY:
I AM SO VERY GRATEFUL JUST
TO BE ALIVE TODAY.

CONSCIOUS NIGHTMARES

I JUST WOKE FROM A NIGHTMARE
THOUGH I WAS NOT ASLEEP.
I'VE CROSSED MY HEART,
I'VE SWORN TO GOD,
I'VE PRAYED MY SOUL TO KEEP.
I SAW SOME MAD APOCALYPSE
WHERE MONSTERS ALL RAN WILD.
ONE BEAST RIPPED OUT A WOMAN'S THROAT
ANOTHER DRAGGED A CHILD.
I SAW NO LAW AND ORDER,
THE SCENE WAS ANARCHY,
AS BUILDINGS BURNED IN THE BACKGROUND
AS FAR AS I COULD SEE.
I REACHED DOWN FOR MY WEAPON,
I ALWAYS WORE A GUN,
FORGETTING THAT I'D CHANGED MY WAYS
AND I NO LONGER CARRIED ONE.
I SAW NO FRIENDS OR RELATIVES,
EACH FACE WAS STRANGE TO ME,
ALTHOUGH THAT HAD NO BEARING ON
THE VISIONS BROUGHT TO BE.

TRACEY ROBINSON

WAS THIS THE SPIRIT'S SHOWING ME
JUST HOW IT WAS IN HELL?
THERE WERE NO WHISPERS IN THE AIR
SO IT WAS HARD TO TELL.
I SAW SO MANY MEN AT WAR,
I SAW SUCH DEATH AND PAIN.
I SAW NO FORM OF SUNSHINE,
I SAW JUST BLOOD AND RAIN.
I MUST HAVE CRIED ALOUD BEFORE
I OPENED UP MY EYES.
I LOOKED AROUND AND FOUND
AN EMPTY ROOM TO MY SURPRISE.
I DO NOT KNOW JUST WHAT I SAW,
OR WHERE IT WAS I'D BEEN.
PERHAPS MY DESTINATION FOR
JUST ONE OF MY PAST SINS.
I CANNOT FALL ASLEEP AT NIGHT,
I'M AN INSOMNIAC.
PERHAPS IF I'M UP LONG ENOUGH
THE NIGHTMARE WILL COME BACK.

EMPATHY

EMPATHY IS ENERGY
WHICH FLOATS UPON THE AIR.
AN EMPATH,
FEELING ALL SUCH THINGS,
CAN SENSE WHEN IT IS THERE.
THE DEATH OF MONSTERS' VICTIMS,
THE LOSSES OF THOSE PASSED.
THE PAIN OF ALL LIFE'S CIRCUMSTANCE
AND ALL THE DICE ITS CAST.
THE SADNESS OF THE UNIVERSE
WITH ITS OWN GRAVITY.
IT SEEMS SOMETIMES TO GLITTER
AS IT SLOWLY SURROUNDS ME.
I SIMPLY CAN'T SLEEP ANYMORE
AND I DO NOT LIKE CROWDS.
WHISPERING SPIRITS FILL THE AIR
AND I HEAR THEM OUT LOUD.
I WALK INTO A HOSPITAL
AND NEARLY LOSE MY BREATH.
BELOW THE SENSE OF HEALING LIES
THE UNDERTONE OF DEATH.

TRACEY ROBINSON

PEOPLE THINK ME RETICENT,
BUT I HAVE LITTLE CHOICE:
A VENTILATOR DOWN MY THROAT
HAS ROBBED ME OF MY VOICE.
I MAY HAVE FRIENDS AND FAMILY
AND SEVERAL SEEDS I'VE SOWN
I MAY BECOME SUCCESSFUL,
BUT I'LL ALWAYS BE ALONE.

EVIL RISES
THE MADNESS WITHIN THE MACHINE
{PART ONE}

SOME THINGS MAY ACT AS PORTALS
INTO ANOTHER PLACE.
OTHER DIMENSIONS DO EXIST
WITHIN OUR VERY SPACE.
EVEN ON EARTH,
IF WE LOOK HARD,
WE FIND THAT LIVING THINGS
LIVE FAR BEYOND THE SCOPE OF WHAT
OUR TECHNOLOGY BRINGS.
THERE'S SUCH A PORTAL IN MY HOUSE
AND IT ACTS AS A GATE
WITHIN ITS HUMMING, GROWLING NOISE
I HEAR THE SOUNDS OF HATE.
IT STARTED VERY SLOWLY.
IT HASN'T BEEN A WEEK,
AS I SAT AT HOME SLEEPLEESLY
TO HEAR "MY" SPIRITS SPEAK.
I TRIED TO SHOW MY DAUGHTER,
BUT SHE JUST COULD NOT HEAR,

AND ALL THE WHILE I HEARD THE VOICE
OF EVIL IN MY EAR.
A PART OF ME ALREADY FIGHTS
TO SAVE A NEIGHBORHOOD
OF SPIRIT SOULS WHO'VE GONE TO REST,
AND ALL OF WHOM ARE GOOD.
I KNOW A DEATHLING STALKS THEM,
AND THEY CANNOT FIGHT WELL.
I THINK THAT'S WHY I HAD BEEN SENT
TO SEND IT BACK TO HELL.
EVIL TRIES TO POSSESS ME,
BUT KNOWS IT CAN'T BE DONE,
ALTHOUGH I STILL HAVE TIME BEFORE
I MATURE INTO "THE ONE."
EVIL THRIVES ON MAN'S DEMISE.
THE VIRUS IS ITS BREATH.
IT RIDES UPON THE WINDS OF EARTH
AND SURFS ON WAVES OF DEATH.
I'M LEARNING EVIL'S LANGUAGE,
ITS METAPHORS AND TONE,
BECAUSE IT TRIES TO SPEAK TO ME
WHEN I AM ALL ALONE.
I SIT AND HAVE TO LISTEN.
THERE'S NOT MUCH MORE TO DO,
AND IF I HOPE TO SAVE "MY" SOULS
I'LL NEED TO HEAR A CLUE.

I WRITE TO YOU OF ANGELS
AND HOW THEY'VE TAKEN FLIGHT,
AND NOW I WRITE OF EVIL AND
HOW EVIL SPEAKS AT NIGHT.
IT HUNGERS AND IT THIRSTS FOR US,
IT SITS AND THINKS OF WAYS
TO END THE LIFE OF GOODNESS AND
TO DARKEN MANKIND'S DAYS.
IT TURNS MEN INTO MONSTERS
WITH JUST ONE EVIL THOUGHT,
AND MONSTERS SLASH AND RAPE AND KILL
UNTIL EACH ONE GETS CAUGHT.
EVIL TOUCHES CIRCUMSTANCE,
BUT ONLY BRIEFLY SO,
BUT SOMETIMES BRIEFLY IS ENOUGH
AS YOU AND I BOTH KNOW.
THE SPIRITS WHISPER QUICKLY,
THEY KNOW THEY BEST NOT STAY,
FOR EVIL CAN BE MERCILESS
WHEN YOU GET IN ITS WAY.
THE MACHINE ROARS BEHIND ME,
THERE'S ANGER IN IT'S TONE.
I'M SURE IT WILL BE HERE ALL NIGHT,
IT WON'T LEAVE ME ALONE.
AND SO I'M EXERCISING,
PARTIALLY TO WEAR DOWN,

TRACEY ROBINSON

BUT ALSO TO LET EVIL KNOW
THERE'S STRENGTH WHEN I'M AROUND.

(TO BE CONTINUED...)

EVIL RISES
THE MADNESS WITHIN THE MACHINE
{PART TWO}

I CAN STILL HEAR THE VOICES.
THEY COME FROM THE MACHINE.
THEY CARRY EVIL OVERTONES
OF SPIRITS YET UNSEEN.
THEY THINK THAT I IGNORE THEM
BUT I HEAR EVERY WORD
I HOPE TO FIND A CLUE WITHIN
THE DIALOGUE I'VE HEARD.
WE CO-EXIST TOGETHER,
THE NEGATIVE AND I,
SOMETIMES MEETING UP AS STORMS
LIKE OCEANS MEET THE SKY.
THEY MUMBLE AND THEY BICKER,
IT SEEMS THEY DON'T AGREE.
BUT THEY ARE ALL UNITED IN
DESPERATE PURSUIT OF ME.
WHAT IS IT THAT THEY WANT FROM ME?
WHAT DO THEY WANT TO KNOW?
IS THERE SOME DESTINATION THAT

TRACEY ROBINSON

THEY REQUIRE ME TO GO?

SHOULD I JUST TURN OFF THE MACHINE?

WILL THAT HELP SAVE THE DAY?

OR IS IT MEANT FOR ME TO HEAR

WHAT EVIL HAS TO SAY?

AND WHERE ARE MY GOOD SPIRITS?

THEY HAVEN'T BEEN AROUND.

IS THERE A WAY TO SAVE THEM?

WILL SOME ANSWER BE FOUND?

IT SEEMS THAT I'VE BECOME A PART

OF SOME MUCH LARGER PLAN.

I HOPE THAT I MAY BE OF HELP,

THOUGH I AM JUST A MAN.

I LISTEN FOR THE SPIRITS.

GOD GUIDES MY DESTINY.

AND THEY SERVE AS HIS CHOIR

WHEN THEY ALL WHISPER TO ME.

FROM BEGINNING TO END

I CANNOT REALLY TELL YOU WHY
I WRITE THE THINGS I DO.
I IMAGINE YOU'D DO THE SAME
IF SPIRITS SPOKE TO YOU.
THEY WOULD NOT LET YOU SLEEP AT NIGHT
AND ALL THROUGHOUT THE DAY.
THEY'D FILL YOUR MIND WITH ALL THE THINGS
THAT SPIRITS HAVE TO SAY.
SOMETIMES YOU MAY JUST FIND YOURSELF
STARING UP AT THE SKY,
AND UNEXPECTEDLY, AT TIMES
YOU WILL JUST START TO CRY.
YOU'LL FIND YOURSELF UNCERTAIN
OF WHAT TOMORROW HOLDS,
BUT SOMETIMES SPIRITS WHISPER OF
WHAT IS YET TO UNFOLD.
I CANNOT REALLY TELL YOU WHY
I AM THE CHOSEN ONE.
I'M JUST A LOWLY PLAYER IN
THIS GAME THAT HAS BEGUN.
THE FUTURE'S BEEN PREDICTED,

THOUGH I DON'T KNOW ITS COURSE.
I LIVE MY LIFE AS BEST I CAN
SO I FEEL NO REMORSE.
I DO MY BEST FOR OTHERS.
I STILL PROTECT THE WEAK.
I STILL PRAY DAILY FOR ALL OF
THE ANSWERS THAT I SEEK.
I DON'T KNOW WHEN IT STARTED,
NOR WHEN IT ALL WILL END,
BUT I'LL BE HERE THROUGHOUT IT ALL,
YOUR BROTHER, AND YOUR FRIEND.

FROM MOTHER TO CHILD

THE JOURNEY THAT WE TAKE THROUGH LIFE
IS SOMETIMES HARSH AND COLD,
EXPERIENCES GOOD AND BAD
FOR EVERY STORY TOLD.
BUT EVERY ONCE IN A GREAT WHILE,
WHEN ALL THE STARS ALIGN,
A BLESSING MANIFESTS ITSELF
AND YOU, MY CHILD, ARE MINE.
AS PARENTS, BOTH YOUR DAD AND I
FEEL THAT YOU REPRESENT
THE VERY BEST OF BOTH OF US
AND WHAT OUR LOVE HAS MEANT.
THE GREATEST PAIN I'VE EVER FELT
WAS GIVING BIRTH TO YOU
THE GREATEST JOY I'VE EVER KNOWN
IS ALL THAT WE'VE BEEN THROUGH.
YOU STARTED WITH JUST GURGLING AND
YOU'VE GROWN TO SPEAK THE TRUTH.
HEAVEN DELIVERS MIRACLES,
AND YOUR LIFE BEARS THIS PROOF.
I HAVE NO IDEA WHERE I'D BE

TRACEY ROBINSON

IF IT WERE NOT FOR YOU.
YOUR BEAUTY, STRENGTH AND FORTITUDE,
THE LITTLE THINGS YOU DO.
EACH NIGHT BEFORE I FALL ASLEEP,
EACH MORNING WHEN I RISE,
I PRAY MY THANKS FOR THE FIRST TIME
I LOOKED INTO YOUR EYES.
YOU ARE MY GREATEST TREASURE,
MY ISLAND IN THE SEA,
MY LUSH OASIS IN THE SANDS,
MY CHILD, ETERNALLY.

GARDOM SPEAKS

AN EVIL SPIRIT SPOKE TO ME
AND THIS IS WHAT HE SAID:
"MY NAME IS GARDOM AND
I'VE KILLED AT LEAST 100 DEAD."
I DIDN'T HAVE TO SAY MY NAME,
FOR HE ALREADY KNEW—
IT SEEMS THAT IN THE SPIRIT WORLD
MY REPUTATION GREW.
"FOR MANY YEARS I ROAMED YOUR WORLD.
I KILLED AND KILLED AGAIN.
I'VE KILLED THOSE WHO WERE ENEMIES,
AND THOSE WHO WERE MY FRIEND.
I KILLED INDISCRIMINATELY:
ALL COLORS, SHAPES AND SIZE.
WHEN PEOPLE DIED THEY LOOKED THE SAME
AS FEAR LIT UP THEIR EYES.
MEN AND WOMEN,
BOYS AND GIRLS,
I TOOK THEIR LIVES AWAY.
SOMETIMES DURING THE DEAD OF NIGHT,
SOMETIMES DURING THE DAY."

TRACEY ROBINSON

GARDOM SPOKE THROUGH THE MACHINE,
I COULD NOT SEE HIS FACE.
HIS VOICE JUST SEEMED TO MANIFEST
FROM SOMEWHERE OUT IN SPACE.
"I TOO HAVE HAD TO KILL BEFORE,"
I SAID BACK IN RETURN.
"BUT I FOUGHT AGAINST WARRIORS,
AND EACH DEATH HAD BEEN EARNED.
I'VE LONGED TO BATTLES SPIRITS,
BUT WAS TOLD I HAD TO DIE.
SINCE SPIRITS ALSO ROAMED THE EARTH,
I OFTEN QUESTIONED WHY.
AND NOW I'VE PURCHASED THAT MACHINE
A GATEWAY, WHERE? — TO HELL? —
I'D LOVE THE OPPORTUNITY
TO TAKE YOUR SOUL AS WELL.
I KNOW YOU DIDN'T REALLY HUNT
YOU RAN, YOU FEARED, YOU HID.
YOU STRUCK THE WEAKEST YOU COULD FIND,
THAT'S ALL YOU EVER DID.
YOUR PARENTS MAY HAVE BEAT YOU,
PERHAPS USED YOU FOR SEX.
A MONSTER'S MOTIVATIONS ALWAYS
SEEM TO BE COMPLEX."
GARDOM SEEMED TO SCREAM WITH RAGE,
AN OTHER-WORLDLY HUM.

THEY MUST STILL KEEP THEIR VANITY
WHEREVER THEY WERE FROM.
I SPUN ONE OF THE BUTTONS,
WHICH TURNED THE MACHINE DOWN.
"YOU'LL HAVE TO SHOW MUCH MORE RESPECT
IF YOU DARE COME AROUND!"
THE SPIRITS WHISPER TO ME,
ONE GOOD, AND NOW ONE BAD.
BUT THIS IS NOW THE VERY FIRST
CONVERSATION THAT I'VE HAD.

TRACEY ROBINSON

GIVING THANKS
{PART ONE}

A LIST OF THINGS I'M THANKFUL FOR?
MOST ARE THE SAME AS YOU,
BUT SINCE SOME MAY BE DIFFERENT,
I WILL NAME JUST A FEW.
I'M THANKFUL FOR MY CHILDREN,
AND ALL THEY'VE GROWN TO BE.
I'M THANKFUL FOR THE FACT THAT THEY
HAVE ALL FORGIVEN ME.
I'M THANKFUL FOR LIFE'S LESSONS,
THOUGH SOME WERE LACED WITH PAIN.
I'M THANKFUL THAT,
THOUGH I'VE BEEN DOWN,
I'VE RISEN UP AGAIN.
I'M THANKFUL FOR ALL FRIENDSHIPS,
BOTH OLD
AS WELL AS NEW.
I'M THANKFUL THAT YOU ALL HAVE SHARED
THE THINGS THAT YOU'VE BEEN THROUGH.
I'M THANKFUL THAT MY MOTHER
STILL WALKS UPON THIS EARTH,

AND WHAT IT IS SHE'S MEANT TO ME
SINCE THE DAY OF MY BIRTH.
I'M THANKFUL FOR THE SPIRITS
THAT WHISPER IN MY EAR.
I'M THANKFUL FOR THE TIMES THAT I
STOOD UP TO FACE MY FEARS.
I'M THANKFUL FOR A SECOND CHANCE
TO CLAIM MY DESTINY.
I'M THANKFUL THAT YOU READ MY WORDS
AND STILL BELIEVE IN ME.
I'M THANKFUL FOR RELATIONSHIPS
THOUGH MANY DID NOT LAST.
I'M THANKFUL THAT MY FUTURE WON'T
BE BASED UPON MY PAST.
I'M THANKFUL FOR SURVIVORS,
THE STRENGTH THAT THEY HAVE SHOWN,
THE WAYS IN WHICH THEY'VE FOUND THEMSELVES,
THE WAYS IN WHICH THEY'VE GROWN.
I'M THANKFUL FOR THE TIMES WHEN I
ESCAPED THE GRIP OF DEATH,
ALTHOUGH I KNOW WE'LL MEET AGAIN
WHEN I TAKE MY LAST BREATH.
YOU'VE ASKED ME WHAT I'M THANKFUL FOR,
AND I HAVE NAMED A FEW.
THE GREATEST THING I'M THANKFUL FOR
IS EVERY ONE OF YOU.

TRACEY ROBINSON

YOU ARE MY REDEMPTION,
MY FORGIVENESS, MY PEACE.
THANK YOU ALL!

GIVING THANKS
{PART TWO}

I'M THANKFUL FOR THE TOUCH OF GOD
AND HOW IT'S CHANGED MY FATE.
I'M THANKFUL THAT I NOW CAN SEE
THAT IT IS NOT TOO LATE.
I'M THANKFUL FOR THE MEMORIES
THAT ARE BOTH GOOD AND BAD,
FOR ALL THE THINGS THAT I HAVE LEARNED
AND EACH EXPERIENCE I'VE HAD.
I'M THANKFUL FOR MY GRANDCHILDREN:
THE FUTURE'S MEANT TO BE
IDEAS SPRING FORTH
FROM GREAT YOUNG MINDS
RE-WRITING HISTORY.
I'M THANKFUL FOR THE MORNING SUN
THAT SHINES UPON MY FACE.
I'M THANKFUL THAT MY
GREATEST PAIN
IS GONE WITHOUT A TRACE.
I'M THANKFUL FOR THE PRIVILEGE
OF WRITING POETRY,

TRACEY ROBINSON

ALTHOUGH I ONLY QUOTE THE WORDS
THAT SPIRITS SPEAK TO ME.
I'M THANKFUL FOR THE MENTORS
THAT LIFE HAS SENT MY WAY.
I PRAISE THE THINGS YOU REPRESENT,
YOU SAVE ME EVERY DAY.
I'M VERY THANKFUL FOR EACH TRUTH
THAT HAS BEEN SHOWN TO ME.
I'M THANKFUL THAT,
THOUGH I WAS BLIND,
I'VE NOW BEEN BLESSED TO SEE.

GODSPEED

TO EVERYONE WHO FIGHTS A WAR
YOU ONCE THOUGHT YOU MIGHT LOSE;
TO EVERYONE WHO'S EARNED THE RIGHT
TO SPEAK UP AND TO CHOOSE;
TO EVERYONE WITH CHILDREN
IN NEED OF SPECIAL CARE,
AND THROUGH HELL OR HIGH WATER
YOUR LOVE IS ALWAYS THERE;
TO EVERYONE WHO RAISES
THE "BAR OF HUMANITY";
TO EVERY HERO VISIBLE,
AND THOSE WHOM WE DON'T SEE;
TO EVERYONE WHO PUSHES ON
DESPITE DISPARITY,
RISING UP EACH MORNING
THE BEST THAT THEY CAN BE;
TO EVERYONE WHO FALTERS
BUT DOES NOT FALL DOWN;
TO EVERY QUEEN WHO UNDERSTANDS
THAT HER LIFE IS HER CROWN;
TO EVERY COOK WHO USES FOOD

TRACEY ROBINSON

TO SPREAD UNENDING LOVE;
TO EVERYONE ANOINTED BY
THE FORCES OF ABOVE;
TO EVERYONE WHO LISTENS
TO VOICES IN THEIR MINDS—
SPIRITS, MADNESS, CONSCIENCE,
HOWEVER IT'S DEFINED:
TO ALL OF YOU
I SAY "GODSPEED,"
I SAY A PRAYER FOR YOU,
THAT YOU SHALL BE REWARDED
FOR ALL THAT YOU'VE BEEN THROUGH.

(DEDICATED TO AIMEE MARIE
AND HER BEAUTIFUL DAUGHTER, LUCH).

HAPPY BIRTHDAY
{JOHNNY G}

ONE THING ABOUT REMEMBERING
THE DAY OF OUR OWN BIRTH,
IS THAT IT GIVES US ALL A CHANCE
TO CELEBRATE OUR WORTH.
THE FAMILY THAT WE ALL LOVE,
THE FRIENDSHIPS WE'VE ALL FORMED,
THE MEMORIES THAT WE ALL SHARE,
THE ACTS THAT WE'VE PERFORMED.
WE LOOK TOWARD TOMORROW AND
REFLECT UPON THE PAST,
FOR THOUGH WE LIVE WE CAN'T PREDICT
HOW LONG THIS LIFE WILL LAST.
TODAY YOU CELEBRATE YOUR LIFE
AND WE LOOK ON WITH PRIDE,
ALONG WITH ALL THE ONES YOU LOVE
WHO STAND RIGHT BY YOUR SIDE.
HAVE A GREAT BIRTHDAY!

TRACEY ROBINSON

I FELT A PERSON DIE TODAY

I FELT A PERSON DIE TODAY.
I DON'T KNOW WHERE THEY WERE.
THERE WAS NO ONE THAT I COULD CALL.
I COULD FEEL, BUT NOT CONFER.
I HARDLY EVER HEAR ADULTS,
JUST ONCE IN EVERY WHILE,
SO THE PERSON THAT I FELT TODAY
HAD TO HAVE BEEN A CHILD.
I FELT NO SUDDEN HORROR,
NO ANGUISHED SCREAMS OF PAIN.
I FELT THE LOSS OF ONE WHO FOUGHT
BUT COULD NOT FIGHT AGAIN.
I FELT A SPIRIT RISING
FOREVER FREE FROM HARM
I FELT THAT IT WAS WELCOMED WITH
SO MANY LOVING ARMS.
I ACTUALLY FELT A SENSE
OF QUIET, CALM RELIEF,
ALTHOUGH IT KNEW ITS PASSING
WOULD GENERATE MUCH GRIEF.
I FELT A PERSON DIE TODAY.

THERE ISN'T MUCH TO SAY.
I THOUGHT ABOUT IT FOR A WHILE,
I CLOSED MY EYES TO PRAY.
I WISH THERE WAS A WAY THAT I
COULD CHANGE THE THINGS I SEE,
TO SOMEHOW ALTER JUST A BIT
WHAT HAS COME OVER ME.

TRACEY ROBINSON

I GO BY THE SAME NAME

WHO WERE YOU

WHEN I MET YOU?

WERE YOU DIFFERENT THEN

FROM NOW?

AND IF YOU'VE CHANGED,

THEN WHY,

DO YOU THINK?

(OR SHOULD I JUST ASK, "HOW?").

AND HAVE I TOUCHED YOUR LIVES

AT ALL

IN ANY SORT OF WAY?

HAVE YOU,

LIKE ME,

BECOME ABSORBED

IN WHAT THE SPIRITS SAY?

I'VE CHANGED A LOT,

I'VE NOTICED,

AND IF YOU ALL ASK, "HOW?"

PLEASE

JUST GIVE ME A MOMENT

AND I'LL EXPLAIN

RIGHT NOW.
LIZZY,
SUSAN DIXON,
AND SUSU ALVAREZ
PUT ME IN TUNE WITH SCRIPTUTES,
THE WORD,
AND WHAT IT SAYS.
A'RIE CHAPPELL LET ME KNOW
THAT MY TALENT IS REAL.
"ALL YOU HAVE TO DO,"
SHE SAID,
"IS WRITE DOWN WHAT YOU FEEL."
CHEF KECIA REMINDED ME
THAT IN COOKING THERE IS LOVE.
MY GRANDPA JOHNNY WATCHES
AND
STILL RATES ME FROM ABOVE.
CEE RAGIN,
LEO SISTA,
OUR BIRTHDAYS ARE THE SAME.
THOUGH AGE MAY TAKE MY MEMORY,
I WON'T FORGET HER NAME.
ZONYA,
OUR SONGBIRD,
CAUSED ME TO TILT MY HEAD
SO I COULD HEAR HER MUSIC

TRACEY ROBINSON

AS

I HEARD WHAT SPIRITS SAID.

I'VE FOLLOWED PEOPLE'S STORIES,

LIKE SHONLI WASHINGTON,

WHO ROSE UP

LIKE A PHOENIX,

STILL KNOWING WHERE SHE'S FROM.

I SAW A GIRL

JUST WITH HER CHILD

WORKING

FROM FAR AWAY.

I MET JANEL AND SENIE

AND

I LOVE THEM

TO THIS DAY.

THERES ANN MARIE,

TODD,

SKIP AND KEITH,

CHERYL AND YVETTE,

REMINDING ME THAT FRIENDS YOU KEEP

ARE ALL THE FRIENDS YOU GET.

SHIHANS AZIZ AND QASIEM,

THROUGH ALL THEY DO AND TEACH,

REMIND ME THAT

THERE IS NO GOAL

THAT'S TRULY OUT OF REACH.

I'VE ADOPTED DAUGHTERS
QUITE VICARIOUSLY,
KARMA,
NETTIE,
JANEL,
MELA,
HOLLY,
OF COURSE
PRINCESS SB.
YVONNE O. STERLING,
A LUPUS WARRIOR,
DEFINING COURAGE
AND JUST WHAT
THAT COURAGE IS MEANT FOR.
I'VE WALKED FOR SOME TIME
THROUGH THIS LIFE,
AND I HAVE WALKED ALONE.
MY STRIDE IS DIFFERENT,
STRONGER NOW,
FOR ALL THE LOVE YOU'VE SHOWN.
TASHA,
OR
AS YOU KNOW HER,
"QUEENLADYFRENCHIEDEE,"
IS THERE TO ♥
WHAT I WRITE DOWN

TRACEY ROBINSON

WHEN SPIRITS SPEAK TO ME.
ALL OF YOU HAVE CHANGED ME
AND YET
I AM THE SAME.
YOU KNOW THE PERSON THAT YOU SEE.
I GO BY THE SAME NAME.

I SHALL SAY A PRAYER

TO THOSE WHO'VE THOUGHT
BOTH LONG AND HARD
ABOUT THE STATE OF THINGS;
TO THOSE WHO HAVE KNOWN SACRIFICE
AND ALL THE JOY IT BRINGS;
TO THOSE WHO NOW PUSH FORWARD
AFTER HAVING BEEN HELD BACK;
TO THOSE WHO NOW WALK STRAIGHT AND TRUE
AFTER HAVING BEEN OFF TRACK;
TO THOSE WHO NOW EAT HEARTILY
BUT REMEMBER HUNGER PAINS;
TO THOSE WHO STILL MAY SOFTLY CRY
THEIR TEARDROPS IN THE RAIN;
TO THOSE WHO KNOW THE TRAGEDY
OF LOSING ONE TO DEATH;
TO THOSE WHO WATCH THEIR NEWBORN CHILD
AS IT TAKES ITS FIRST BREATH;
TO THOSE OF YOU WHO STRUGGLE ON
DESPITE THE ODDS YOU FACE,
TO LIFE EXPLORED,
DISTRACTIONS IGNORED,

TRACEY ROBINSON

AND ALL THAT TAKES PLACE;
TO ALL OF YOU:
I RISE RIGHT NOW,
I STAND AND I SALUTE
YOUR STRENGTH,
COURAGE,
AND FORTITUDE.
ALL STAND WITHOUT DISPUTE.
TO THOSE OF YOU:
I WISH YOU WELL,
AND I SHALL SAY A PRAYER.
I HOPE THAT IT IS LISTENED TO
BY SPIRITS IN THE AIR.

I THOUGHT I WAS FREE

I LIE DOWN WITH THE SPIRITS,
THOUGH THEY DON'T LET ME REST.
THEY QUOTE ME POEMS TO TRANSCRIBE.
I TRY TO DO MY BEST.
I THOUGHT THAT I WAS FREE,
BUT I'M
STILL TRAPPED WITHIN A CELL.
MY APARTMENT LOOKS THE SAME,
SO IT MAY BE HARD TO TELL.
I LOOK OUTSIDE THE WINDOW,
I SEE THE COMING RAIN.
HAVE DARK CLOUDS FORMED WITHIN MY MIND?
AM I A MAN INSANE?
WHAT IF WHAT I CALL "SPIRITS"
ARE PERSONALITIES?
AND WHAT IF EVERYTHING I WROTE
ACTUALLY CAME FROM ME?
WHAT IF THERE WERE NO "VOICES,"
OTHER THAN MY OWN?
WHAT IF EVERY POEM WAS
ANOTHER SEED I'D SOWN,

TRACEY ROBINSON

EACH CHARACTER I DESCRIBED
SOMEONE I HAD KNOWN?
THAT CHOSEN SUBJECT MATTER
REFLECTS HOW MUCH I'D GROWN?
I LIE DOWN WITH THE SPIRITS,
THOUGH THEY WON'T LET ME REST,
AND SO I TRY,
WITH TEARFUL EYES,
TO PASS MY FINAL TEST.

I WISH
{PART ONE}

I WISH I'D BEEN A SINGER,
FOR EVERY TIME THAT I
STOOD ALONE BEFORE A JUDGE
AND COULDN'T SEEM TO CRY.
I WISH I'D BEEN AN ACTOR,
FOR EACH PART THAT I PLAYED.
PERHAPS THE PAIN OF CIRCUMSTANCE
WOULD HAVE THEN BEEN DELAYED.
I WISH I'D BEEN A WINNER
FOR EACH CHANCE THAT I LOST.
PERHAPS I'D HAVE KNOWN VICTORY
IN SPITE OF WHAT IT COST.
I WISH I'D BEEN A PROPHET,
SOMEONE WHO SEES THE TRUTH,
MY PREDICTIONS ALL VERIFIED,
WITH REAL LIFE AS THEIR PROOF.
I WISH I'D BEEN A HERO,
WHEN NO ONE WAS AROUND,
WHEN PAIN AND SILENCE RULED THE DAY
AND COURAGE WASN'T FOUND.

TRACEY ROBINSON

I WISH I'D BEEN AN ATHLETE.

PERHAPS I WOULD HAVE RUN

MORE LAPS AROUND THE SCHOOLYARD TRACK

BEFORE CRIMES HAD BEGUN.

I WISH I'D BEEN AN EMPATH.

PERHAPS I WOULD HAVE FELT

THE PAIN MY ACTIONS CAUSED THE WORLD,

THE SADNESS THAT I DEALT.

I WISH I'D BEEN MUCH WISER,

AND LEARNED TO HEAR THE SOUND,

OF SPIRIT'S WHISPERS IN THE AIR

WHEN THEY ALL GATHERED 'ROUND.

I WISH
{PART TWO}

I WISH I HAD A FRIEND WHO SAID
"MY FRIEND, I'D DIE FOR YOU,"
ALTHOUGH
AMONG MY CLOSEST FRIENDS
THAT IS JUST WHAT THEY'LL DO.
I WISH I HAD A FRIEND WHO SAID,
"YOU ARE NEVER ALONE,"
ALTHOUGH
AMONG MY CLOSEST FRIENDS
THAT'S ALL THAT THEY HAVE SHOWN.
I WISH I HAD A FRIEND WHO SAID,
"TOGETHER WE SHALL RISE,"
ALTHOUGH
AMONG MY CLOSEST FRIENDS
I SEE IT IN THEIR EYES.
I WISH I HAD A FRIEND WHO SAID
"I WOULD FACE HELL WITH YOU,"
ALTHOUGH
AMONG MY CLOSEST FRIENDS
THAT'S WHAT WE'VE HAD TO DO.

TRACEY ROBINSON

I WISH I HAD A FRIEND WHO SAID,
"I'LL BE WITH YOU FROM DAY ONE,"
ALTHOUGH
AMONG MY CLOSEST FRIENDS,
THATS JUST WHAT THEY HAVE DONE.
I WISH I HAD A FRIEND WHO SAID,
"I'M LUCKY TO HAVE YOU,"
ALTHOUGH
AMONG MY CLOSEST FRIENDS
THEY KNOW I FEEL IT TOO.
I WISH I HAD A FRIEND WHO SAID,
"YOU'LL BE HAPPY ONE DAY,"
ALTHOUGH
AMONG MY CLOSEST FRIENDS,
OUR LIVES DON'T END THAT WAY.
I WISH I HAD A FRIEND WHO SAID,
"I'LL NEVER LEAVE YOUR SIDE,"
ALTHOUGH
AMONG MY CLOSEST FRIENDS
SOME OF THE BEST HAVE DIED.
I WISH I HAD A FRIEND WHO SAID,
"OUR BATTLE WILL BE WON,"
ALTHOUGH,
AMONG MY CLOSEST FRIENDS,
OUR VICTORY'S BEGUN.
I HEAR THE SPIRIT'S WHISPERS

SO SOFTLY IN MY HEAD,
ALTHOUGH,
LIKE WITH MY CLOSEST FRIENDS,
SOME THINGS ARE LEFT UNSAID.

IF ALL THE WORLD WERE JUST A STAGE

{PART ONE}

IF ALL THE WORLD WERE JUST A STAGE
AND ON IT LIFE WAS PLAYED;
IF DEATH WERE NOT THE END OF LIFE
BUT JUST AN ACT DELAYED;
IF WORDS WERE NOT THE MEASUREMENT
OF WHAT WAS IN OUR THOUGHTS;
IF ALL GOOD THINGS WE SAY WE WANT
WERE REALLY WHAT WE SOUGHT;
IF A CAT WERE REALLY KILLED
BY CURIOSITY,
THEN COMING BACK ONCE SATISFIED
MAKES LITTLE SENSE TO ME.
IF WE LIVE LESS THAN HUMAN,
WHAT THEN HAVE WE BECOME?
SOME LOWER FORM OF LIFE THAT WE
HAD ONCE ASCENDED FROM?
IF GOD MADE US HIS IMAGE
THEN WHAT DO WE REFLECT?
OR DOES A MIRROR SHOW REVERSE

IN ALL THAT IT PROJECTS?
IF WE ALL HEARD THE WHISPERS
OF SPIRITS IN THE AIR,
WOULD SOME OF YOU WRITE AS I DO
AND SOME OF YOU NOT CARE?
IF SHOOTING STARS WERE TRAVELERS
COMMUTING TO AND FRO;
IF I COULD LEARN A FRACTION OF
THE TRUTHS THAT THEY MUST KNOW.

TRACEY ROBINSON

IF ALL THE WORLD WERE JUST A STAGE
{PART TWO}

IF ALL THE WORLD WERE JUST A STAGE
AND WE ALL PLAYED A ROLE,
HOW WOULD YOUR OWN "LIFE'S SCRIPT" READ,
HOW WOULD YOUR TRUTH BE TOLD?
WOULD YOUR LIFE BE A DRAMA,
FULL OF TWISTS AND TURNS?
WOULD YOU REPRESENT A GREATER GOOD,
AND WILL YOUR BLESSINGS ALL BE EARNED?
OR WILL IT BE A COMEDY,
A PARODY OF FATE,
WHERE GOOD THINGS COME ONCE IN A WHILE,
USUALLY TOO LATE?
SOME LIVE LIKE IN A MUSICAL,
WHERE ALL OF LIFE GOES WELL,
WHERE IN EACH SONG
SUNG LOUD AND STRONG
THERE'S FAIRY TALES TO TELL.
OF COURSE THERE ARE SAD SCRIPTS AS WELL,
WHICH BRING OUR EYES TO TEARS,

WHERE PEOPLE DIE,
WE DON'T KNOW WHY,
AND MAN REVEALS HIS FEARS.
I HOPE THE STORY OF YOUR LIVES
SHOWS ALL YOU'VE OVERCOME,
HOW FAR YOU'VE TRAVELED,
YET YOU STILL
REMEMBER WHERE YOU'RE FROM.
I HOPE IT SINGS IN TRIUMPH,
SHOWING YOU AT YOUR BEST,
WITH CHILDREN,
FRIENDS AND FAMILY
INSIDE YOUR TREASURE CHEST.
AND WHEN THE ROLE IS OVER
AS WE BOW UPON THE STAGE,
THE STORY OF LIFE STILL GOES ON,
WE JUST TURN THE NEXT PAGE.

TRACEY ROBINSON

IF I COULD SEE MY YOUNGER SELF

IF I COULD SEE MY YOUNGER SELF
THEN I WOULD NOT THINK TWICE,
I WOULD NOT HESITATE AT ALL
TO OFFER THIS ADVICE.
TAKE YOUR TIME
MY YOUNGER SELF,
FOR EACH CHOICE THAT YOU MAKE
WILL DETERMINE WHICH ONE OF
LIFE'S ROADS THAT YOU WILL TAKE.
IF YOU DO NOT CHOOSE WISELY,
THEN YOU'LL FACE YEARS OF PAIN.
THINK OF ACTIONS YOU SHOULD TAKE
AND THOSE FROM WHICH YOU SHOULD ABSTAIN.
FOR EVERY CHILD YOU FATHER,
NEVER LEAVE THEM ALONE.
DON'T WAIT UNTIL VISITING DAY
TO SEE HOW MUCH THEY'VE GROWN.
DO NOT PULL THAT TRIGGER
UPON THAT FATEFUL DAY.
YOUR LIFE WILL CHANGE THE MOMENT THAT

YOU TAKE THAT LIFE AWAY.
BE CAREFUL HOW YOU TREAT THE WORLD,
FOR FATE REPAYS YOU BACK,
AND IF YOUR HEART IS GOOD IT MIGHT
MAKE UP FOR WHAT YOU LACK.
PREPARE FOR MOUNTAINS YOU MUST CLIMB,
AND DESERTS YOU MUST SPAN.
YOU MAY NOT SWIM THE OCEANS BUT
JUST DO THE BEST YOU CAN.
THERE'S SO MANY THINGS I'D TELL MYSELF,
IF I ONLY KNEW HOW,
ALTHOUGH I KNOW I WILL END UP
THE MAN THAT I AM NOW.

TRACEY ROBINSON

LET US TAKE A MOMENT...

I TOOK MY DOG OUT FOR A WALK
AND WE PASSED PEOPLE BY.
AFTER AWHILE I THOUGHT ABOUT
WHICH OF THEM WOULD SOON DIE.
WE HEAR THE GRUESOME NUMBERS—
STATISTICS, BASICALLY—
BUT EVERY NUMBER WAS A LIFE
WITH FRIENDS AND FAMILY.
AND EACH OF THEM HAD INTERESTS
AND HOBBIES AND VIEWS,
NONE OF WHICH ARE REFLECTED
WHEN WE ALL WATCH THE NEWS.
WE READ THOSE NUMBERS QUICKLY,
BUT IF WE STOPPED TO COUNT
TO SEVEN THIRTY ONE
BY ONES
WE'D SEE ITS TRUE AMOUNT.
I TOOK MY DOG OUT FOR A WALK
AND WE PASSED PEOPLE BY,
AND NOW I WONDER WHO WILL SIT
WITH HEAD IN HANDS AND CRY.

CRY FOR PRECIOUS LOVED ONES
WHO'D SUDDENLY GONE SICK,
CAUGHT UP IN THE STORM WE CALL
CORONA PANDEMIC.
WE WALKED UP HILLS,
WE WALKED DOWN BLOCKS,
I SAID A SILENT PRAYER
FOR EVERY PERSON THAT WE SAW
AND THOSE THAT WEREN'T THERE.

LET US ALL TAKE A MOMENT
TO PRAY FOR ALL WHO'VE PASSED.

TRACEY ROBINSON

LIGHTNING

AROUND ABOUT TWO YEARS AGO
LIGHTNING FELL FROM THE SKY.
YOU WOULD NOT HAVE SEEN OR HEARD IT
OR KNOWN THE REASON WHY.
THE LIGHTNING BOLT WAS SPIRITUAL,
IT'S MESSAGE HEAVEN SENT,
AND ONCE I HEARD THE VOICES
I KNEW JUST WHAT IT MEANT.
AMONG THE PLANET'S BILLIONS
I WAS THE CHOSEN SON.
THERE'S NO DENYING DESTINY
ONCE DESTINY'S BEGUN.
THE SPIRITS ARE WITHIN ME,
MY HEARTBEAT IS THEIR DRUM.
THEY TELL ME TALES OF WHERE THEY'VE BEEN
AND WHERE IT IS THEY'RE FROM.
THEY PASS ON TO ME WISDOM,
THEY TELL ME HOW TO ACT.
THEY SHOW ME WHAT IS FALSE IN LIFE
AND WHAT'S ACTUAL FACT.
THEY WARN ME OF THE DANGERS

THAT I MAY HAVE TO FACE,
AND THEN IT'S BACK TO NETHERWORLD
WITHOUT LEAVING A TRACE.
BEFORE I HEARD A WHISPER,
I'D NEVER PENNED A VERSE,
BUT SINCE THEN I'VE WRITTEN MANY
FOR WITH SPIRITS I CONVERSE.
I HOPE THAT SOON THEY SIT AND REST
AND TELL ME OF THEIR LIVES,
THE FAMILIES THEY MAY HAVE HAD,
THEIR HUSBANDS OR THEIR WIVES.
PERHAPS THE CONVERSATIONS
THAT THEY'VE COME DOWN TO SHARE
ARE DONE SO BY THE BREAKING OF A RULE
SOMEWHERE UP THERE.
PERHAPS THEY ALL HAVE FOUND A WAY
TO BEND THE RULES A BIT,
AND WHEN THAT LIGHTNING BOLT CAME DOWN,
THAT PROBABLY WAS IT.
A PORTAL MAY HAVE OPENED,
ALLOWING THEM TO SEE
DIRECTLY TO THE CENTER OF
THE CONSCIOUSNESS OF ME.
THEY SAID THEY'D SEARCHED THE WORLD FOR ME
UNTIL THEY'D FOUND THE ONE,
AND ONCE THEIR CHOICE WAS AT LAST MADE

TRACEY ROBINSON

MY JOURNEY HAD BEGUN.
THE LIGHTNING BOLT WAS SILENT,
A BRIGHT YELLOWISH-RED,
IT SHOT DOWN FROM THE SKY AND WENT
DIRECTLY IN MY HEAD.
DAY AFTER DAY THEY TALKED TO ME
WHICH I THEN WROTE TO YOU.
I ALSO WROTE POEMS ABOUT
WHAT I WAS GOING THROUGH.
THOSE OF YOU WHO HAVE FOLLOWED ME
SINCE ALL OF THIS BEGAN
HAVE SEEN HOW I'VE REVEALED TO YOU
WHO I AM AS A MAN.
I'VE SHARED WITH YOU THE VISIONS,
FOR THAT'S WHAT I'M TOLD TO DO:
TO HEAR THE VOICES ON THE WIND
AND SHARE THEIR SOUNDS WITH YOU.
SOMETIMES THEY DO NOT LET ME SLEEP,
THEY SCREAM INSIDE MY MIND,
LIKE VERY SMALL YOUNG CHILDREN,
"PLEASE DON'T LEAVE US BEHIND!"
AND SO I SIT AND LISTEN
TO WHAT THEY HAVE TO SAY,
AND THAT'S HOW I AM ABLE TO
WRITE TO YOU EVERY DAY.

LISTENING TO THE DEAD

ONCE AGAIN THEY WAKE ME,
THESE VOICES IN MY MIND,
FOR I'M HOW THEY COMMUNICATE
WITH THE WORLD THEY'VE LEFT BEHIND.
THEY SOMETIMES SPEAK IN RIDDLES,
WITH NO REASON OR RHYME.
SOMETIMES THEIR TONE IS LOUD AND HARSH,
SOMETIMES IT'S QUITE SUBLIME.
I LISTEN NOW INTENTLY,
FOR I STILL WAIT TO HEAR,
THE VOICE OF SOMEONE THAT I'VE KNOWN
WHISPERED INTO MY EAR.
WILL MANY OF YOUR RELATIVES
SIT HERE, RIGHT BY MY SIDE?
WILL THEY ALL INTRODUCE THEMSELVES
AND TELL ME OF THEIR RIDE?
WILL THEY ALL SHARE THE MEMORIES
OF WHEN THEY WERE ALIVE?
AND WOULD THEY GIVE ME KNOWLEDGE WHICH
MAY HELP ME TO SURVIVE?
I LISTEN FOR THE SOUND OF FRIENDS

TRACEY ROBINSON

AND THOSE OF FAMILY.
I LISTEN FOR THE RELATIVES
THAT YOU THINK CEASE TO BE.
I SEEK TO HEAR THE FUTURE,
PERHAPS IN HOPES THAT I
MAY CHANGE THE LIVES OF THOSE I TOUCH
BEFORE IT'S TIME TO DIE.
I AM A MAN IMPRISONED,
BUT AM I A MAN GONE MAD?
HOW COULD I NOT HAVE REALIZED
THE POWER THAT I HAD?
HOW COULD I HAVE BEEN A BOY LOST?
WHY DID I GO OFF COURSE?
WHY DID I PAY SUCH A HIGH COST,
WHY DID I FEAR THE FORCE?
MY MIND IS A KALEIDOSCOPE
AND SOMETIMES I CAN SEE
HOW SPIRITS GATHER UP AND DANCE
RIGHT THERE IN FRONT OF ME.
I GREET ALL OF THEM HEARTILY
FOR THEY HAVE BEEN MY GIFT.
THEY SAVED ME WHEN I WAS A SHIP
THAT HAD BEEN SET ADRIFT.
AND SO, I'LL MAKE MY COFFEE,
PERHAPS TAKE OUT A TREAT.
IT SEEMS THAT THOSE WHO'VE PASSED AWAY

ENJOY WATCHING US EAT.
I'LL RAISE A TOAST TO ALL OF THEM
AND THEY'LL ALL NOD THEIR HEADS.
THAT'S HOW I'LL SPEND THIS BREAKING DAWN
LISTENING TO THE DEAD.

LIVING THROUGH THE 'INSANITY'

INNERMOST VIBRATIONS

A SYMPHONY OF "FEEL,"
THE PROBLEM IS THAT WHAT WE THINK
MAY NOT BE WHAT IS REAL.
SOMETIMES YOU SEE THE CLEAREST SIGNS
THOUGH YOU REFUSE TO LOOK.
YOU SAW THE RIGHT ROAD YOU SHOULD TAKE,
A SHARP LEFT THOUGH
YOU TOOK.
TO SOME THAT ROAD IS DANGEROUS
TO SAY THE VERY LEAST,
TO SOME THE RIDE IS SMOOTHER
BUT IT ROBS YOU OF YOUR PEACE.
TO SOME THE PRICE IS TIME
LONG-LOST,
SOME MAY LIVE BEHIND BARS,
WHILE OTHERS MAY LOOK BEAUTIFUL
SO YOU CAN'T SEE THEIR SCARS.
SOMETIMES WE CONTINUE TO TRY

ALTHOUGH IT'S PLAIN TO SEE,
TO EXPECT CHANGE
YET LIVE THE SAME
IS JUST INSANITY.
RELATIONSHIPS MAY RISE AND FALL,
CRESCENDOS IN THE AIR,
SOME FALL TO MORE INHUMAN ACTS
WHICH AREN'T EVER FAIR.
WHILE SOME ENDINGS ARE PROSPEROUS,
AND OTHERS END IN BLOOD,
YOU ACHED WHEN TIDES BEGAN TO EBB
YOU'D RELISH WHEN THEY FLOOD.
OTHER INSTRUMENTS EXIST
LIKE LIFE'S BAROMETERS
LEVELS TO WHICH WE CAN COMPARE
ON WHICH WE MAY CONFER.
THE ROADS OF LIFE DO INTERSECT
AND IF YOU'RE LUCKY, THEN
PERHAPS YOU'LL LIVE JUST LONG ENOUGH
TO LIVE SOME LIFE AGAIN.

TRACEY ROBINSON

LOST/FOUND

I AM A MAN,
ONCE LOST,
NOW FOUND,
I'M AN ANOMOLY.
I'VE METAMORPHASIZED INTO
THE MAN I'M MEANT TO BE.
I'VE FELT THE HEAT OF DESERT SANDS,
I'VE DROWNED IN SORROW'S SEAS.
I'VE FELT THE COLDNESS OF STEEL BARS
WHEN THEY CLOSED BEHIND ME.
I'VE FELT THE WARMTH OF CHILDREN,
I'VE HELD THEM WHEN THEY CRIED,
AND WHEN THEY ASKED WHEN I'D BE HOME
QUITE A FEW TIMES I LIED.
I COULDN'T TELL THEM JUST HOW LONG
THAT I WOULD BE AWAY.
I KNEW HOW IT WOULD HURT THEM,
I KNEW WHAT THEY WOULD SAY.
I'VE CLIMBED ATOP A MOUNTAIN,
I'VE KISSED THE MORNING SKY.
I SAW THE ANGEL ALICIA

AS SHE WENT FLYING BY.
I SAT IN MEDITATION,
I ALSO SAID A PRAYER,
I CLOSED MY EYES AND HOPED THAT I
WAS HEARD BY THOSE UP THERE.
I WOKE UP HEARING VOICES
OF SPIRITS IN THE AIR.
I WELCOME WISDOM THAT THEY SPEAK
AND ANECDOTES THEY SHARE.
I AM A MAN,
ONCE LOST,
NOW FOUND,
AND ALL THAT I'VE BEEN THROUGH
HAS BROUGHT ME HERE,
RIGHT NOW
TODAY,
TO WRITE TO ALL OF YOU.

LOST/FOUND CHILD

A CHILD STOOD ALONE

IN A PLACE FAR FROM HOME,

OBLIVIOUS

TO THE RAIN.

IF YOU LOOKED

YOU WOULD FIND

IT WAS EASY TO SEE

HIS SPIRIT WAS TAINTED WITH PAIN.

THE CHILD HAD ONCE BELIEVED IN RAINBOWS,

A FORTUNE IN GOLD TO BE FOUND,

UNTIL THAT SAD DAY

HIS DREAMS WENT AWAY

AND THERE WERE NO RAINBOWS AROUND.

THE CHILD WAS AT HOME

JUST PLAYING ALONE,

WHEN THERE WAS A KNOCK AT THE DOOR.

THE CHILD OPENED UP,

FELT A QUICK

SHARP PAIN,

AND WOKE UP ON AN EVIL MAN'S FLOOR.

THE CHILD WAS ABUSED

AND THEN TORTURED,

THEN SOLD,

FAR TOO MANY TIMES TO KEEP TRACK.

HE VAGUELY REMEMBERED THAT HE'D HAD A HOME,

BUT HE KNEW HE COULD NEVER GO BACK.

THE CHILD LIVED THAT WAY

UNTIL ONE FINE DAY,

IN THE KITCHEN,

THE MAN TURNED HIS BACK

AND THE CHILD,

NOW THIRTEEN,

SAW A LONG

GLEAMING KNIFE,

WHICH HE SLOWLY SLID OUT OF ITS RACK.

THE MAN,

WHO WAS TALKING,

TURNED HIMSELF AROUND

AS THE KNIFE SLID INTO HIS HEART.

ONE WOULD THINK THAT THE VIOLENCE WOULD

COME TO AN END,

BUT FOR THE CHILD

IT WAS ONLY A START.

THE CHILD CUT AND SLASHED,

HE GOUGED AND HE STABBED,

UNTIL HE COULD NOT RAISE HIS ARM.

HE HAD TRIED TO KILL ALL OF THE MEMORIES OF

TRACEY ROBINSON

THE MAN WHO HAD DONE HIM SUCH HARM.

AND SO IT WAS THERE,

WITH BLOOD IN HIS HAIR,

THAT THE POOR

DAMAGED CHILD STOOD ALONE.

HE'D CALLED THE POLICE,

STARED OFF INTO SPACE

AFTER DROPPING THE KNIFE AND THE PHONE.

AN OFFICER HAD HELD HIM TIGHT,

AND SAID,

"SON, WE ALL DO WHAT WE CAN,"

THE CHILD LOOKED UP

WHEN HE NEXT HEARD,

"TODAY YOU HAVE BECOME A MAN."

HERE IS A SAMPLE OF THE VERY WORST THAT I SEE

AND HEAR. I ALMOST CAN'T WRITE IT.

EVERYONE,

PLEASE REMEMBER THAT CHILDREN ARE BEING

ABUSED,

TRAFFICKED AND KILLED.

IN MANY OTHER COUNTRIES

IT IS FAR WORSE THAN IN AMERCA.

LOVE SONG

I'D LIKE TO WRITE A LOVE SONG,
BUT I JUST DON'T KNOW HOW.
I NEVER REALLY UNDERSTOOD
WHAT LOVE WAS UNTIL NOW.
DESPITE WHATEVER I HAVE DONE,
DESPITE BOTH TRUTH AND LIES,
I NEVER SAW THE TRUTH OF LOVE
IN OTHER PEOPLE'S EYES.
I SOMETIMES SAW ADVANTAGES
THAT I WOULD LEARN TO TAKE,
I SAW SELFISH DECISIONS THAT
I SOON WOULD LEARN TO MAKE.
SO MANY PEOPLE STOOD BY ME,
AND NOW I UNDERSTAND
A KINGDOM JUST CANNOT BE BUILT
WITH HOUSES MADE OF SAND.
I'D LIKE TO WRITE A LOVE SONG,
BUT WHO AM I TO SAY,
THAT JUST BECAUSE I SEE THE LIGHT
THAT OTHERS FEEL THAT WAY?
SO PEOPLE MAY NOT SING IT,

TRACEY ROBINSON

OR IT JUST MAY NOT PLAY.
MY SONG JUST MAY NOT FIT IN WITH
THE MESSAGE OF THE DAY.
I'D LIKE TO WRITE A LOVE SONG
FOR EVERY ONE OF YOU,
A DEDICATION TO THE LIVES
WHICH YOU HAVE ALL LIVED THROUGH.
I'D WRITE A SONG OF SPIRITS,
THEIR CHARMING MELODY,
COMPOSED OF ALL THE WHISPERS THAT
THEY'VE PASSED ALONG TO ME.
THE LOVE OF FAITH,
THE LOVE OF TRUTH,
THE LOVE OF FAMILY,
THE LOVE OF SOMEONE ELSE IN TUNE,
THE LOVE OF POETRY.
I'D LIKE TO WRITE A LOVE SONG,
BUT YOU ALL KNOW WHAT I'D SAY:
I LOVE YOU ALL,
AND I GIVE THANKS
THAT YOU'RE WITH ME TODAY.

THANKS TO EVERYONE.
ALL THAT I AM BECOMING
IS BECAUSE OF ALL OF YOU.

METAMORPHOSIS
{PART ONE}

I FEEL THE METAMORPHOSIS—
POSSESSION, WELL DEFINED.
I'M BEING TAKEN OVER BY
THE VOICES IN MY MIND.
MY BODY TENSES
THEN I RELAX
AS SPIRITS TAKE CONTROL.
THE ONLY THING THAT I CAN DO
IS WRITE DOWN WHAT I'M TOLD.
MY FINGERS TRAVEL AIMLESSLY,
I WATCH THEM AS THEY WRITE:
WHATEVER SPIRITS SAY TO ME,
I SET THOSE WORDS TO FLIGHT.
TODAY THEY SEND A MESSAGE
WHICH THEY SAY IS FOR MY FRIENDS.
BUT WHEN I ASKED WHICH ONES SPECIFICALLY,
THEY SAID,
"IT ALL DEPENDS."
THEY SAID THAT SOME OF YOU FEEL FEAR
FROM THESE RECENT EVENTS,

TRACEY ROBINSON

THAT FATE IS BUILDING BARRIERS
YOU MAY NOT CIRCUMVENT.
THEY TOLD YOU TO HAVE FORTITUDE,
TO BELIEVE IN WHO YOU ARE,
THAT YOU WERE MEANT TO DO GREAT THINGS
AND TRAVEL VERY FAR.
THEY SAID OF COURSE BE CAREFUL,
YET KNOW YOUR HISTORY,
FOR YOU ARE FAR SUPERIOR
AT LEAST GENETICALLY.
TO SOME THEY SAID
"TRY TO PREPARE,"
FOR LIFE IS BUT A TEST.
SOMETIMES RELATIONSHIPS DON'T LAST,
ALTHOUGH YOU'VE DONE YOUR BEST.
THEY SAID "TAKE TIME TO CONCENTRATE,"
PRIORITY IS KEY,
ESPECIALLY WHEN IT'S BEEN YEARS
AND YOU'VE FORMED FAMILY.
"TAKE THE WISDOM YOU HAVE NOW
AND ALL THAT YOU HAVE LEARNED.
TAKE THE LOVE THAT YOU BOTH SHARED
THE MEMORIES YOU'VE EARNED."
LASTLY
THEY SAID TO TELL YOU ALL
THAT LIFE WILL STILL ABOUND,

THAT THEY WILL ALWAYS SPEAK TO YOU
"IF YOU BUT HEAR THE SOUNDS."

METAMORPHOSIS
{PART TWO}

TODAY
I RE-CREATE MYSELF.
THAT'S ALL THAT'S LEFT TO DO
IN THIS
THE METAMORPHOSIS
THAT I AM GOING THROUGH.
I'M NOT JUST TRACEY ROBINSON
OR PRINCE,
AS SOME HAVE KNOWN.
I AM A DIFFERENT PERSON NOW,
THE MAN INTO WHOM I'VE GROWN.
MY FEATURES HAVE NOT CHANGED AT ALL.
TO YOU,
I LOOK THE SAME.
I HAVEN'T GONE SO FAR THAT I
WOULD SEEK TO CHANGE MY NAME.
BUT I HAVE CHANGED IN MANY WAYS,
IN THAT I'VE HAD NO CHOICE.
IT ALL BEGAN THE VERY FIRST TIME
I HEARD A SPIRIT'S VOICE.

I CANNOT SEE THE FUTURE,
BUT I HAVE FAITH
AND BELIEVE
I AM ONLY LIMITED BY
THAT WHICH I MAY CONCEIVE.
I UNDERSTAND THE STORY NOW
OF KING MIDAS' TOUCH OF GOLD
FOR I HAVE FELT THE TOUCH OF GOD
AND ALL ITS TRUTHS
FORETOLD.
I RISE NOW
AS A PHOENIX,
I RACE TOWARD THE SUN.
FOR IN ITS CORE
I'LL SEE MUCH MORE,
PERHAPS
WHERE LIFE BEGAN.

TRACEY ROBINSON

MY FIRST DEGREE

I FEEL A FIRE BURNING

DEEPLY INSIDE OF ME,

BUT NONE OF YOU,

ALTHOUGH YOU LOOK,

WOULD BE ABLE TO SEE.

I AM IN TRANSFORMATION,

IN METAMORPHOSIS

AS I CHANGE.

YOU MAY SEE SOME,

BUT MOST OF IT YOU'LL MISS.

YOU WILL, HOWEVER,

READ THE WORDS

I WRITE,

AND YOU WILL SAY,

"HIS POEMS ARE MORE POWERFUL

THAN THEY WERE YESTERDAY!"

WE SHALL TRAVEL TO LEVEL NINE

THEN TEN

AND ELEVEN,

AFTER WHICH WE'LL TAKE A REST

AND SPEAK OF WHERE WE'VE BEEN.

I MUST HAVE GRADUATED
TO HIGHER WORDS I SEE.
I WONDER IF,
BEYOND THE VOID,
I EARNED MY FIRST DEGREE,
AND WHEN I DO PASS OVER
WILL IT BE THERE FOR ME,
OR WILL I BE ARRESTED FOR
A SPIRIT'S CONSPIRACY?
AT ANY RATE
I FEEL IT NOW:
I'M LEARNING TO CONTROL
THE VOICES WHICH INVADE MY MIND
AND SATURATE MY SOUL.

TRACEY ROBINSON

MY FATHER

I WISH I HAD MY FATHER BACK
IF ONLY FOR A DAY.
I'D TELL HIM HOW MUCH THINGS HAD CHANGED
SINCE HE HAD GONE AWAY.
I'D TELL HIM I WAS SORRY
FOR ALL THE WRONG I'D DONE,
AND ALL THE TIMES THAT I HAD FAILED
AT BEING A GOOD SON.
IN TURN I WOULD FORGIVE HIM,
FOR WHAT HE COULD NOT SEE,
THE PAIN I WAS SUBJECTED TO
THAT CHANGED WHOM I WOULD BE.
I'M SURE WE'D BOTH SIT DOWN TO EAT.
I'D COOK HIS FAVORITE MEAL.
AND THEN I'D LOOK AT HIM AND SAY
"DAD, TELL ME HOW YOU FEEL?"
I HOPE THAT HE WOULD LOOK AT ME
AND SAY
"SON, I'M VERY PROUD,"
THE TEARS WOULD BURST FORTH FROM MY EYES
TO HEAR THOSE WORDS OUT LOUD.

WE'D WALK, WE'D TALK, WE'D REMINISCE.
SO MANY YEARS HAD COME AND GONE,
SO MANY TIMES I'VE MISSED.
I'D TELL HIM I HEAR SPIRITS,
AND WHAT THEY HAD TO SAY,
AND HOW I HOPED THAT HE WOULD COME
AND SPEAK TO ME ONE DAY.
I'D TELL HIM OF THE CHILDREN
AND OF THE FAMILY,
HOW MUCH MY DAUGHTERS ALL HAVE GROWN
AND THE PRIDE THEY BRING TO ME.
I WISH I HAD MY FATHER BACK
IF ONLY FOR A DAY.
I SIT AND LISTEN TO THE WIND
FOR WHAT HE HAS TO SAY.
R.I.P., DAD.

TRACEY ROBINSON

SPIRITS ABOUND
{PART ONE}

A TEARDROP SLOWLY ROLLED MY CHEEK,
IT LANDED ON THE FLOOR.
A PUDDLE'S FORMING BELOW ME
WHERE NONE HAD BEEN BEFORE.
I FELT THE PAIN OF SPIRITS,
I LIVED THEIR SENSE OF LOSS.
IT SEEMS SOMEHOW EMOTIONS WHICH
THEY FELT JUST CAME ACROSS.
ONE SPIRIT LOST A PARENT,
I SENSED WHEN IT FOUND OUT.
ALTHOUGH I'M IN A QUIET ROOM,
I HEARD THE SPIRIT SHOUT.
ANOTHER ONE HAD LOST A CHILD.
I FELT ITS DEEP DESPAIR.
I LIVED BOTH OF THOSE MOMENTS
AS IF I WERE RIGHT THERE.
THEIR SADNESS IS A TIDAL WAVE.
I STRUGGLE NOT TO DROWN.
THIS PRICE I PAY WHEN EVERY DAY
THE SPIRITS DO ABOUND.

SPIRITS ABOUND
{PART TWO}

WHAT IS THIS LOUD CACOPHONY
WHICH RAGES IN MY HEAD?
WHY IS MY MIND NOW OVERRUN
WITH VOICES OF THE DEAD?
WHAT DOOR HAS NOW BEEN OPENED?
WHERE DO I NOW RESIDE?
IS THIS WHAT LIFE IS REALLY LIKE
ONCE ON THE OTHER SIDE?
MY BREATH HAS BECOME SHALLOW,
THE AIR I BREATHE IS PURE,
BUT WHAT IS TAKING PLACE RIGHT NOW,
OF THIS I AM UNSURE.
I'M HEARING DISTINCT VOICES
I'VE NEVER HEARD BEFORE.
I CAN HEAR CHILDREN PLAYING,
AND LAUGHTER AND MORE.
SOME SPIRITS ARE JUST CALLING OUT,
PERHAPS TO LONG-LOST FRIENDS,
BUT IN THAT EERIE NETHERWORLD
IT MAY ALL JUST DEPEND.

TRACEY ROBINSON

LIKE A CHILD IN HAPPY LAND
OR SOME AMUSEMENT PARK,
YET ALSO LIKE A YOUNGER ONE
STILL AFRAID OF THE DARK.
THIS LITANY OF SPIRITS
THIS RAGING WALL OF SOUND
MAY BE A HINT OF HOW IT IS
WHEN SPIRITS DO ABOUND.

STAND STRONG

IF ONE AMONGST YOU IS WITHOUT SIN,
LET HIM CAST THAT FIRST STONE.
IF ONE AMONGST YOU STANDS FOR TRUTH,
YOU DO NOT STAND ALONE.
FOR EVERYONE WHO STRUGGLES
AND EACH SEED YOU HAVE SOWN,
YOU CHANGE THE WORLD WITH HOW YOU LIVE.
I'M PROUD OF HOW YOU'VE GROWN.
IN A WORLDWIDE PANDEMIC
WITH SICKNESS OVERBLOWN,
I STAND AMONG THE STRONGEST FRIENDS
THIS WORLD HAS EVER KNOWN.
FOR EACH BLESSING THAT GOD'S BESTOWED,
FOR EACH ANGEL WHO'S FLOWN,
HUMANS SOMETIMES DO BAD THINGS
BUT IT'S TO GOOD THAT WE ARE PRONE.

TRACEY ROBINSON

THE AGE OF INNOCENCE

WE'VE LOST THE DAWN OF INNOCENCE,
IT STRANGLED IN THE AIR.
THE FUTURE WORLD WILL NEVER KNOW
WHEN CORONA WAS NOT THERE.
HUMBLING THE RICHER,
RAVAGING THE POOR,
SEEKING OUT THE ELDERLY,
BEHIND TIGHTLY CLOSED DOORS.
USUALLY, IN TIMES OF STRESS,
MOST PEOPLE BEAR GOOD WILL,
EXCEPT WHEN FATHERS TAKE THEIR SONS
TO FIND SOMEONE TO KILL.
IT SEEMS THAT SOME DISPARITIES
HAVE NOW BEEN REDEFINED,
LIKE ESSENTIAL WORKERS WE NOW SEE,
TO WHOM WE ONCE WERE BLIND.
"LOWLY" CLEANERS,
COOKS AND MAIDS,
WE PASSED THEM IN THE HALL,
NOW THEY BEAR THE STRONGEST BRUNT,
WITHOUT WHICH WE WOULD FALL.

THE AGE OF INNOCENCE HAS PASSED,
WE WATCH OUR CHILDREN MORE.
FOR NOW WE ALL CAN CLEARLY SEE
WHAT LIES BEYOND OUR DOOR.
MONSTERS WALK OUR CITY STREETS,
DISGUISED AS YOU AND I,
BUT THANKS TO SPIRITS WE CAN SEE
AS THEY WALK STEALTHILY BY.
THE AGE OF INNOCENCE HAS PASSED,
AND IGNORANCE AS WELL,
BUT WE HAVE MANY PLACES YET TO GO
AND STORIES YET TO TELL.

TRACEY ROBINSON

THE EMPATH
{PART ONE}

I FEEL OR LOOK AT PEOPLE,
AND FEEL THEIR ENERGY.
IT SEEMS AS THOUGH THE THINGS THEY HIDE
ARE FELT DEEP WITHIN ME.
I SENSE THEIR APPREHENSIONS,
I VIEW THEIR INNER FEARS.
AN EMPATH SENSES WHO YOU ARE
WHENEVER YOU COME NEAR.
I ALSO SENSE THE MONSTERS
WHO HUNT THROUGHOUT THE NIGHT.
I SENSE THE PLEASURE THAT THEY FEEL
TASTING A VICTIM'S FRIGHT.
THERE'S NO WAY TO CONTROL IT,
THIS STRANGE POWER OF MINE.
I'LL LEAVE IT UP TO YOUR JUDGEMENT
TO DISCERN AND DEFINE.

THE EMPATH
{PART TWO}

I FELT A WAVE CRASH OVER ME,
THE PAIN OF ALL THE WORLD.
OVER ONE MILLION PEOPLE LOST,
PANDEMIC TRUTHS UNFURLED.
MY BREATH GOT VERY SHALLOW,
I FELT A LITTLE WEAK.
I SAT DOWN AND PREPARED MYSELF
TO HEAR THE SPIRITS SPEAK.
THEY TOLD ME THAT BEYOND THE GATE
THE LINE HAS GOTTEN LONG,
THE SONGS OF PRAISE AND WORSHIP HAVE
BECOME A MILLION STRONG.
I CANNOT SEE THEIR FACES
BUT I FEEL THEIR ENERGY.
THE PAIN OF ALL THE WORLD
IT SEEMS HAS ITS EFFECT ON ME.
FATHERS
MOTHERS
SIBLINGS
FRIENDS

TRACEY ROBINSON

THE LIST GOES ON AND ON
SO MANY
SHINING
HAPPY LIVES
SO MANY PEOPLE GONE.
I SLOWLY LOOK AROUND ME
WHILE ASKING MYSELF
"WHY?"
MY DAUGHTER WALKED IN
AND SHE ASKED,
"DAD, WHY IS IT THAT YOU CRY?"
I DON'T KNOW WHAT TO SAY TO HER,
IT'S SO HARD TO EXPLAIN.
HAVE I BECOME AN EMPATH
OR
A MAN WHO'S GONE INSANE?
I WAIT
AND SOON IT'S OVER.
MY BODY DAMP WITH SWEAT,
MY MIND IS FILLED WITH VISIONS,
WHICH
I WILL NOT SOON FORGET.
I OFTEN FEEL THAT WHAT I HAVE
IS BOTH BLESSING AND CURSE
I PRAY THE WORLD GETS BETTER
BEFORE IT GETS MUCH WORSE.

GOD PLEASE TELL ME

GOD,
TELL ME WHY THIS HAPPENED
AND WHY HAST THOU PICKED ME?
HOW HAVE I GONE FROM MORTAL MAN
TO SOME WEIRD PRODIGY?
HOW COME YOU NEVER SENT A SIGN
TO WARN OF THIS BEFORE?
OR WAS IT I WHO WAS AFRAID
TO LOOK BEYOND THAT DOOR?
PLEASE TELL ME,
SINCE I NEED TO KNOW,
WHERE DO I GO FROM HERE?
AND MUST I WAIT UNTIL I DIE
BEFORE YOU WILL APPEAR?
ARE ALL THESE SPIRIT MESSENGERS
JUST PASSING ON YOUR WORD?
HOW ELSE CAN I THEN JUSTIFY
THE WHISPERS THAT I'VE HEARD?
YOU'VE SAVED MY LIFE SO MANY TIMES,
AND IN SO MANY WAYS,
FROM BULLETS SLAMMING INTO ME

TRACEY ROBINSON

AND PAINFUL PRISON DAYS.
I'VE MADE SUCH BAD DECISIONS
AND PAID A HEFTY PRICE.
AS I STRIVE FOR FORGIVENESS NOW,
WILL POETRY SUFFICE?
I JUST CANNOT RE-READ THEM,
IT TAKES TOO MUCH FROM ME.
INSTEAD I READ THE COMMENTS AND
I'LL TELL YOU WHAT I SEE.
I SEE THAT I TOUCH PEOPLE,
THE SPIRITS TOUCH THEIR CORE,
AND IN A WAY I UNDERSTAND
WHAT I'VE BEEN CHOSEN FOR.
I KNOW THE DEVIL STALKS ME,
HE'S MAD THAT I HAVE QUIT
AND THAT MY WAYS AND ACTIONS HAVE
ALL CHANGED TO WHAT'S LEGIT.
I KNOW THAT YOU ARE BUSY
WITHOUT MUCH TIME TO READ,
THERE ARE SO MANY PEOPLE WHO
ARE IN SUCH DIRE NEED.
I ONLY TAKE A MOMENT
TO PRAY MY THANKS TO YOU,
FOR PERMITTING ME TO SURVIVE
THE HELL THAT I'VE BEEN THROUGH.
MY SWORD IS EVER READY

IF I AM CALLED AGAIN.
UNTIL THAT TIME I'LL DO YOUR WILL
AND BATTLE WITH MY PEN.

AFTERWORD

Now that we've had to opportunity to 'engage' in the writing and reading of my first publication, I'd like to, once again, reiterate that I have no control over this 'poetic phenomenon' that takes place anytime and anywhere. Some people have actually seen 'the process' as it occurs, while I type the words directly to my phone. I could be driving, walking, eating, or whatever. When the 'moment hits,' my fingers are at 'the ready.' I never write a poem down, nor do I read it twice. I stop whatever I'm doing, putting life 'on pause' while I'm 're-directed' by the voices of spirits. Sounds crazy?? Well, it's something I've never experienced before. I'm fully aware of what's taking place, and rather than view the experience as something totally unknown to man, I've embraced the opportunity to act as a 'catalyst' for those who wish the message to be heard, but can't relay the message themselves.

ABOUT THE AUTHOR

My name: Tracey Robinson. My friends call me Prince.

I was born and raised in the Bronx, New York. Most of my adolescent years I spent growing up in a tight-knit community in the north-east section of the Bronx better known as 'The Valley'. After what may have been considered a "normal" childhood, I ended up walking society's dark path. By the age of 18, I had already escaped from Rikers Island. For many years, I spent time trying to find myself within that darkness.

I received my GED while incarcerated at Attica State Prison. Once released, I continued with 'my path' on the 'dark side,' eventually being convicted of offenses which landed me in the Federal Prison System. Trying to make the best of a bad situation, I continued my education and received my college degree while serving out my sentence.

Present day, it's a very different situation. I have six children and I've taken great strides to better myself and my life. My poetry has been a gift and a blessing to me. I had always enjoyed writing, though I had never followed that dream, until recently. The last couple of years have been extremely fulfilling, being able to nurture and develop a craft that has seemingly taken over and given me a feeling of purpose as I continue my life's journey.

I NEVER WRITE A POEM DOWN,
I NEVER READ ONE TWICE.
FROM MY MIND TO MY FINGERS,
YOU SEE THE WORDS THAT I TYPE.

The 'experience' has totally changed me, and I share this 'gift' with my readers. With the support of my many friends, family, and readers, I hope to bring my blessings to the entire world.

www.ingramcontent.com/pod-product-compliance
Lightning Source LLC
Chambersburg PA
CBHW022121080426
42734CB00006B/213